SCHOLASTIC

PR1ME

Mathematics

3B

Coursebook

For information regarding permission, write to:
Scholastic Education International (Singapore) Pte Ltd
81 Ubi Avenue 4, #02-28 UB.ONE, Singapore 408830
Email: education@scholastic.com.sg

For sales enquiries, write to:

Latin America, Caribbean, Europe (except UK),
Middle East and Africa
Scholastic International
557 Broadway, New York, NY 10012, USA
Email: intlschool@scholastic.com

New Zealand
Scholastic New Zealand Ltd
Private Bag 94407, Botany, Auckland 2163
Email: orders@scholastic.co.nz

India
Scholastic India Pvt. Ltd.
A-27, Ground Floor, Bharti Sigma Centre,
Infocity-1, Sector 34, Gurgaon 122001, Haryana, India
Email: education@scholastic.co.in

Australia
Scholastic Australia Pty Ltd
PO Box 579, Gosford, NSW 2250
Email: scholastic_education@scholastic.com.au

United Kingdom
Scholastic Ltd
Euston House, 24 Eversholt Street, London NW1 1DB
Email: education@scholastic.co.uk

Rest of the World
Scholastic Education International (Singapore) Pte Ltd
81 Ubi Avenue 4, #02-28 UB.ONE, Singapore 408830
Email: education@scholastic.com.sg

Visit our website: www.scholastic.com.sg

First edition 2014
Reprinted 2014, 2016

ISBN 978-981-07-3296-7

About PR1ME Mathematics

Welcome to **Scholastic PR1ME™ Mathematics**.

The program covers the five strands of mathematics across six grades: **Numbers and Operations**, **Measurement**, **Geometry**, **Data Analysis**, and **Algebra (Grades 5 and 6)**.

Numbers and Operations

Data Analysis

Measurement

Geometry

Each chapter of the Coursebook comprises three parts, **Let's Remember**, **Lessons**, and **Practice**.

1. **Let's Remember** offers an opportunity for systematic recall and assessment of prior knowledge in preparation for new learning.

Each item is carefully crafted to help check for readiness to receive new knowledge.

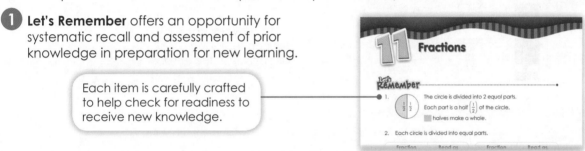

2. Each chapter contains **lessons**, each focusing on a concept or an aspect of it. Concepts and skills are introduced in **Let's Learn**, and **Let's Do** provides opportunities for immediate formative assessment.

In **Let's Learn**, concepts and skills are introduced and developed to mastery using the *concrete-pictorial-abstract* approach. This proven, research-based approach develops deep conceptual understanding.

Let's Do provides opportunities for formative assessment. Systematic variation of tasks reinforces students' understanding and enables teachers to check learning and identify remediation needs.

Practice Book links lead to exercises in the Practice Book to further reinforce understanding of the concepts and skills learnt.

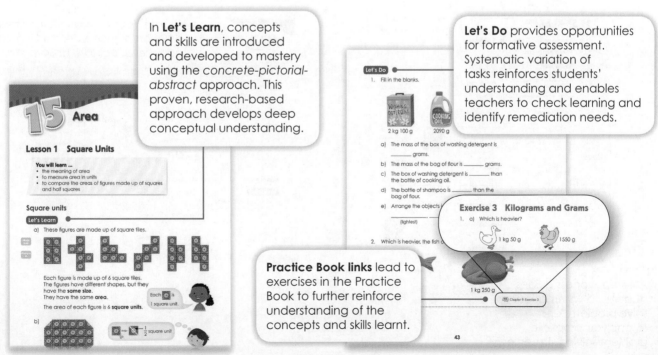

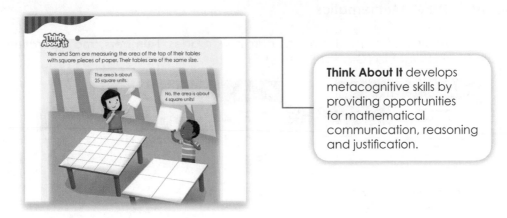

Think About It develops metacognitive skills by providing opportunities for mathematical communication, reasoning and justification.

3 **Practice** provides opportunities for summative assessment and independent practice.

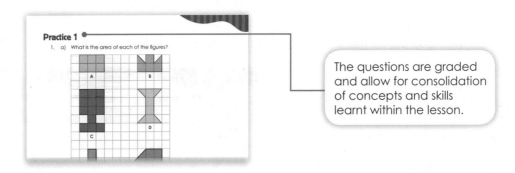

The questions are graded and allow for consolidation of concepts and skills learnt within the lesson.

Chapters end with a **Problem Solving** lesson.
Word problems provide a meaningful context for students to apply mathematical knowledge.
The focus is on both the strategies and the process of problem solving.

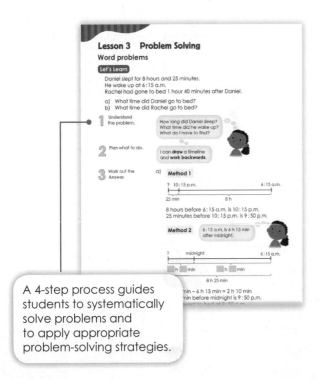

A 4-step process guides students to systematically solve problems and to apply appropriate problem-solving strategies.

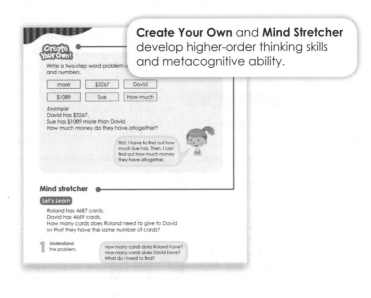

Create Your Own and **Mind Stretcher** develop higher-order thinking skills and metacognitive ability.

Contents

Chapter 8 Length

Let's Remember 7
Lesson 1:   Meters and Centimeters 9
Practice 1 15
Lesson 2:   Kilometers 16
Practice 2 23
Lesson 3:   Millimeters 24
Practice 3 30
Lesson 4:   Problem Solving 31
Practice 4 33

Chapter 9 Mass

Let's Remember 35
Lesson 1:   Kilograms and Grams 37
Practice 1 46
Lesson 2:   Problem Solving 48
Practice 2 51

Chapter 10 Volume and Capacity

Let's Remember 53
Lesson 1:   Volume 55
Practice 1 59
Lesson 2:   Liters 60
Practice 2 66
Lesson 3:   Liters and Milliliters 68
Practice 3 76
Lesson 4:   Problem Solving 77
Practice 4 79

Chapter 11 Fractions

Let's Remember 82
Lesson 1:   Fraction of a Whole 84
Practice 1 86
Lesson 2:   Equivalent Fractions 87
Practice 2 94
Lesson 3:   Adding Fractions 95
Practice 3 98
Lesson 4:   Subtracting Fractions 99
Practice 4 102
Lesson 5:   Problem Solving 103
Practice 5 105

Chapter 12 Time

Let's Remember ·· 108
Lesson 1: Hours and Minutes ················· 110
Practice 1 ·· 125
Lesson 2: Other Units of Time ················ 126
Practice 2 ·· 129
Lesson 3: Problem Solving ····················· 130
Practice 3 ·· 133

Chapter 13 Geometry

Lesson 1: Angles ··································· 135
Practice 1 ·· 141
Lesson 2: Right Angles ·························· 142
Practice 2 ·· 144
Lesson 3: Problem Solving ····················· 145

Chapter 14 Perpendicular and Parallel Line Segments

Let's Remember ·· 146
Lesson 1: Perpendicular Line Segments ····· 147
Practice 1 ·· 153
Lesson 2: Parallel Line Segments ············ 154
Practice 2 ·· 159
Lesson 3: Horizontal and Vertical Line Segments ····· 161
Practice 3 ·· 162
Lesson 4: Problem Solving ····················· 163

Chapter 15 Area

Lesson 1: Square Units ·························· 165
Practice 1 ·· 169
Lesson 2: Area in Square Centimeters and
           Square Meters ······················· 171
Practice 2 ·· 176
Lesson 3: Problem Solving ····················· 178

Glossary ·· 180

Problem Solving Process ······················· 184

Length

1.

John   sister   mother   father

John is shorter than 1 meter.

His father is  1 meter.

His mother is ▨ his sister.

The meter is a unit of length. We use meter (m) for longer or taller objects.

7

2.

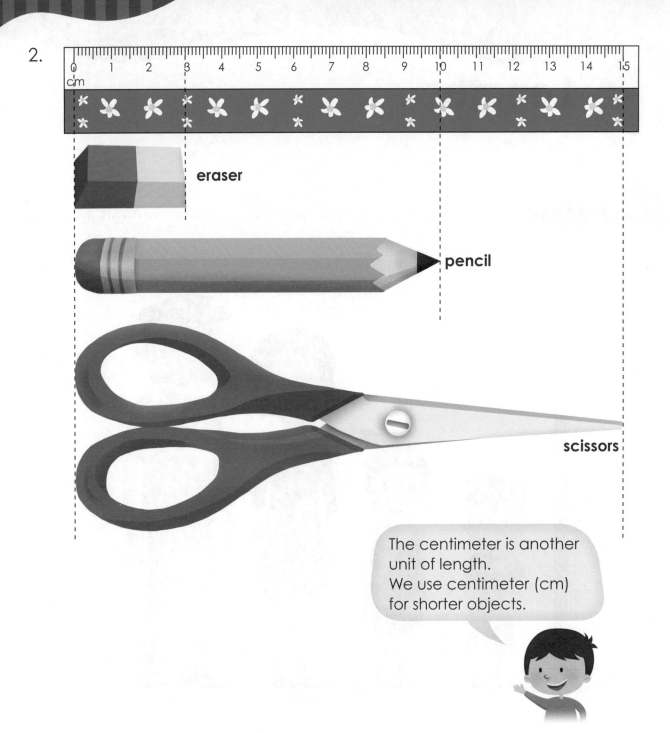

The centimeter is another unit of length.
We use centimeter (cm) for shorter objects.

The eraser is 3 centimeters long.

The pair of scissors is ▢ centimeters long.

The pencil is 5 centimeters shorter than the pair of scissors.

The pencil is ▢ centimeters longer than the eraser.

Lesson 1   Meters and Centimeters

You will learn to...
- measure and compare lengths in meters and centimeters
- express meters and centimeters in centimeters
- express centimeters in meters and centimeters
- add and subtract lengths in meters and centimeters

Length in meters and centimeters

Let's Learn

Sue is measuring the length of her guitar with a meter ruler.
Her guitar is as long as the meter ruler.

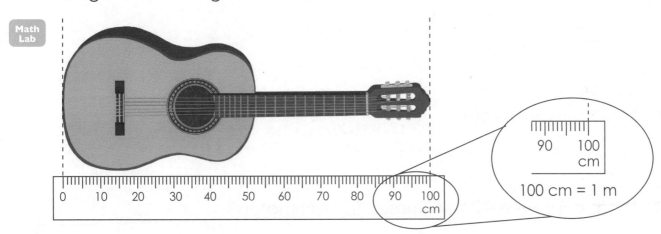

100 cm = 1 m

Sue's guitar is 1 meter or 100 centimeters long.

| 1 meter = 100 centimeters |
| 1 m = 100 cm |

1 meter is 100 times as long as 1 centimeter.

Estimate the length of the whiteboard in your classroom. Then, check by measuring it with a meter ruler.

Is the length closer to 2 meters or 3 meters?

1. Walk five steps. Measure the distance with your meter ruler. Is the distance more than or less than 3 meters? _____

Expressing meters and centimeters in centimeters

Let's Learn

a) Ali's height is 1 meter 25 centimeters. What is his height in centimeters?

1 m 25 cm is ☐ cm more than 1 m.

1 m 25 cm ⟨ 1 m = 100 cm
         25 cm

1 m 25 cm = 100 cm + 25 cm
        = 125 cm

Ali's height is 125 centimeters.

b) What is 2 meters 72 centimeters in centimeters?

2 m 72 cm ⟨ ☐ m = ☐ cm
          ☐ cm

1 m = 100 cm
2 m = ☐ cm

2 m 72 cm = ☐ cm + ☐ cm
        = ☐ cm

Let's Do

1. Express in centimeters.

    a) 1 m 90 cm = _____ cm   b) 1 m 55 cm = _____ cm

    c) 2 m 86 cm = _____ cm   d) 2 m 89 cm = _____ cm

    e) 3 m 8 cm = _____ cm   f) 4 m 6 cm = _____ cm

Expressing centimeters in meters and centimeters

Let's Learn

a) A car is 395 centimeters long.
What is its length in meters and centimeters?

$$395 \text{ cm} \begin{cases} 300 \text{ cm} = 3 \text{ m} \\ 95 \text{ cm} \end{cases}$$

100 cm = 1 m

395 cm = 3 m + 95 cm
= 3 m 95 cm

The length of the car is 3 meters 95 centimeters.

b) What is 145 centimeters in meters and centimeters?

$$145 \text{ cm} \begin{cases} \boxed{} \text{ cm} = \boxed{} \text{ m} \\ \boxed{} \text{ cm} \end{cases}$$

145 cm = ☐ m + ☐ cm
= ☐ m ☐ cm

Let's Do

1. Express in meters and centimeters.

a) 180 cm = _____ m _____ cm

b) 195 cm = _____ m _____ cm

c) 262 cm = _____ m _____ cm

d) 299 cm = _____ m _____ cm

e) 304 cm = _____ m _____ cm

f) 409 cm = _____ m _____ cm

Comparing lengths in meters and centimeters

Let's Learn

The table shows the heights of two basketball players.

Name	Height
Mark	189 cm
Rami	2 m 8 cm

Who is taller?

Express the heights in centimeters.

2 m 8 cm $\Big\langle$ 2 m = 200 cm
            8 cm

2 m 8 cm = 200 cm + 8 cm
         = 208 cm

208 cm is greater than 189 cm.
So, Rami is taller than Mark.

My father is 1 meter 78 centimeters tall.

Yen

My father is taller!
He is 175 centimeters tall.

Sam

Is Sam correct? Explain why.

Let's Do

1. Arrange the lengths in order.
    Begin with the longest.

    | 3 m 5 cm | 360 cm | 3 m 55 cm |

    _____, _____, _____
    (longest)

 Chapter 8: Exercise 1, pages 7–8

Adding and subtracting meters and centimeters

Let's Learn

Lily has a red ribbon 3 meters 60 centimeters long and
a yellow ribbon 1 meter 20 centimeters long.

a) What is the total length of the ribbons?

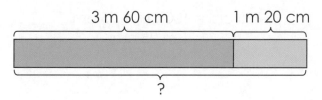

3 m 60 cm   1 m 20 cm

?

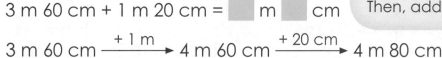

3 m 60 cm + 1 m 20 cm = ▢ m ▢ cm

First, add the meters.
Then, add the centimeters.

3 m 60 cm $\xrightarrow{+\ 1\ m}$ 4 m 60 cm $\xrightarrow{+\ 20\ cm}$ 4 m 80 cm

The total length of the ribbons is 4 meters 80 centimeters.

b) How much longer is the red ribbon than the yellow ribbon?

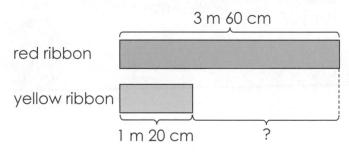

3 m 60 cm

red ribbon

yellow ribbon

1 m 20 cm   ?

3 m 60 cm – 1 m 20 cm = ▢ m ▢ cm

First, subtract the meters.
Then, subtract the centimeters.

3 m 60 cm $\xrightarrow{-\ 1\ m}$ 2 m 60 cm $\xrightarrow{-\ 20\ cm}$ 2 m 40 cm

The red ribbon is 2 meters 40 centimeters longer than
the yellow ribbon.

Let's Do

1. Add or subtract.

   a) 2 m 15 cm + 4 m 35 cm = _____ m _____ cm

   b) 5 m 80 cm – 3 m 45 cm = _____ m _____ cm

a) 4 m 40 cm + 1 m 85 cm = ☐ m ☐ cm

Method 1

 4 m 40 cm $\xrightarrow{+\ 1\ m}$ 5 m 40 cm $\xrightarrow{+\ 85\ cm}$ 5 m 125 cm = 6 m 25 cm

125 cm = 100 cm + 25 cm
= 1 m 25 cm

Method 2

4 m 40 cm ⟨ 4 m = 400 cm / 40 cm

1 m 85 cm ⟨ 1 m = 100 cm / 85 cm

4 m 40 cm + 1 m 85 cm = 440 cm + 185 cm
= 625 cm
= 6 m 25 cm

600 cm = 6 m

b) 4 m 40 cm − 1 m 85 cm = ☐ m ☐ cm

Method 1

4 m 40 cm $\xrightarrow{-\ 1\ m}$ 3 m 40 cm $\xrightarrow{-\ 85\ cm}$?

2 m 140 cm $\xrightarrow{-\ 85\ cm}$ 2 m 55 cm

Method 2

4 m 40 cm − 1 m 85 cm = 440 cm − 185 cm
= 255 cm
= 2 m 55 cm

1. Add or subtract.

   a) 1 m 58 cm + 70 cm = _____ m _____ cm

   b) 2 m 95 cm + 2 m 45 cm = _____ m _____ cm

   c) 3 m – 2 m 35 cm = _____ m _____ cm

   d) 4 m 5 cm – 1 m 85 cm = _____ m _____ cm

P/B Chapter 8: Exercise 2, pages 9–11

Practice 1

1. Express in centimeters.

   a) 4 m
   b) 1 m 40 cm
   c) 2 m 25 cm
   d) 3 m 95 cm
   e) 4 m 8 cm
   f) 9 m 9 cm

2. Express in meters and centimeters.

   a) 120 cm
   b) 252 cm
   c) 309 cm
   d) 618 cm
   e) 963 cm
   f) 405 cm

3. Arrange the lengths in order. Begin with the shortest.

   680 cm   6 m 85 cm   6 m 58 cm   608 cm

4. Subtract.

   a) 1 m – 65 cm
   b) 1 m – 55 cm
   c) 2 m – 1 m 75 cm
   d) 2 m – 95 cm
   e) 3 m – 2 m 95 cm
   f) 3 m 40 cm – 6 cm

5. Add or subtract.

   a) 2 m 75 cm + 3 m
   b) 3 m 4 cm + 65 cm
   c) 1 m 26 cm + 2 m 65 cm
   d) 4 m 8 cm + 1 m 95 cm
   e) 5 m 85 cm – 5 cm
   f) 5 m 90 cm – 76 cm
   g) 2 m 55 cm – 1 m 50 cm
   h) 3 m 6 cm – 2 m 25 cm

Lesson 2 Kilometers

You will learn to...
- measure and compare lengths in kilometers
- express kilometers and meters in meters
- express meters in kilometers and meters
- add and subtract lengths in kilometers and meters

Length in kilometers

Let's Learn

The **kilometer** is a unit of length.
We write **km** for kilometer.

A train carriage is about 10 meters long.
The total length of 100 train carriages is about 1 kilometer.
1 kilometer is 1000 times as long as 1 meter.

> 1 kilometer = 1000 meters
> 1 km = 1000 m

We measure long distances in kilometers.

16

Look at the picture below.

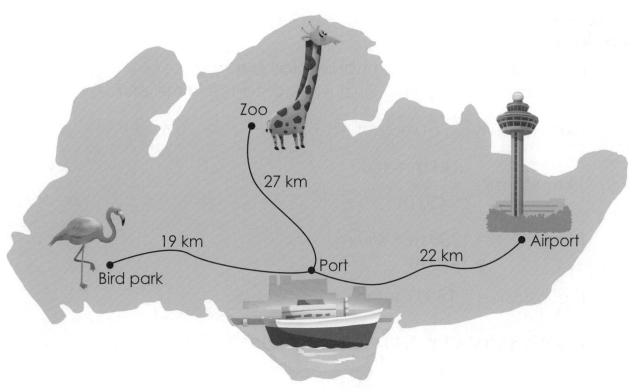

a) The distance from the zoo to the port is 27 kilometers.

b) The distance from the bird park to the airport
   is ▊ kilometers.

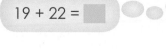

$19 + 22 =$ ▊

Let's Do

1. Fill in the blanks with **centimeters**, **meters** or **kilometers**.

   a) The distance from my home to the airport is

      about 42 _____.

   b) The length of my hand is about 12 _____.

   c) The length of my bed is about 2 _____.

P/B Chapter 8: Exercise 3, pages 12–13

Expressing kilometers and meters in meters

Let's Learn

a) The distance from Adam's house to his school is 1 kilometer 450 meters. What is the distance in meters?

1 km 450 m is ▢ m more than 1 km.

1 km 450 m ⟨ 1 km = 1000 m
            450 m

1 km 450 m = 1000 m + 450 m
           = 1450 m

The distance is 1450 meters.

b) What is 8 kilometers 848 meters in meters?

8 km 848 m ⟨ ▢ km = ▢ m
             ▢ m

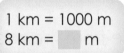

8 km 848 m = ▢ m + ▢ m
           = ▢ m

1 km = 1000 m
8 km = ▢ m

Let's Do

1. Express in meters.

a) 1 km 600 m = _____ m

b) 2 km 550 m = _____ m

c) 2 km 605 m = _____ m

d) 3 km 85 m = _____ m

e) 3 km 20 m = _____ m

f) 4 km 5 m = _____ m

18

Expressing meters in kilometers and meters

Let's Learn

a) The Golden Gate Bridge in the U.S. is 2737 meters long. What is its length in kilometers and meters?

2737 m
- 2000 m = 2 km
- 737 m

1000 m = 1 km

2737 m = 2 km + 737 m
      = 2 km 737 m

The length of the Golden Gate Bridge is 2 kilometers 737 meters.

b) What is 1078 meters in kilometers and meters?

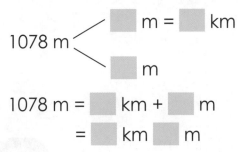

1078 m
- ☐ m = ☐ km
- ☐ m

1078 m = ☐ km + ☐ m
      = ☐ km ☐ m

Let's Do

1. Express in kilometers and meters.

a) 1830 m = ____ km ____ m   b) 2304 m = ____ km ____ m

c) 2780 m = ____ km ____ m   d) 3096 m = ____ km ____ m

e) 3040 m = ____ km ____ m   f) 4009 m = ____ km ____ m

19

Comparing lengths in kilometers and meters

Let's Learn

The table shows the lengths of some of the world's longest bridges.

Name	Length
Sharavathi Bridge	2 km 60 m
Thanh Tri Bridge	3 km 84 m
Tsing Ma Bridge	2 km 200 m

Which bridge is the longest?
Which bridge is the shortest?

 2 km 60 m = ☐ m

3 km 84 m = ☐ m

2 km 200 m = ☐ m

The ☐ Bridge is the longest.

The ☐ Bridge is the shortest.

Express the lengths in meters. First, compare the thousands. 3 thousands is greater than 2 thousands. So, the Thanh Tri Bridge is the longest.

Next, compare the hundreds 0 hundreds is smaller than 2 hundreds. So, the Sharavathi Bridge is the shortest.

Let's Do

1. Arrange the distances in order. Begin with the shortest.

| 4 km 400 m | 4 km 404 m | 4004 m | 4 km 40 m |

_____, _____, _____, _____
(shortest)

P/B Chapter 8: Exercise 4, pages 14–15

Comparing lengths in kilometers and meters

Adding and subtracting kilometers and meters

Let's Learn

Zoe took part in a race. She had to cycle
3 kilometers 400 meters and run 1 kilometer 650 meters.

a) What is the total distance of the race?

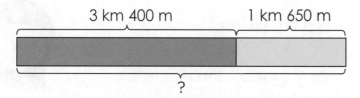

3 km 400 m + 1 km 650 m = ▭ km ▭ m

Method 1

First, add the kilometers.
Then, add the meters.

3 km 400 m $\xrightarrow{+\ 1\ km}$ 4 km 400 m $\xrightarrow{+\ 650\ m}$ 4 km 1050 m = 5 km 50 m

1050 m = 1000 m + 50 m
= 1 km 50 m

Method 2

3 km 400 m ⟨ 3 km = 3000 m
400 m

1 km 650 m ⟨ 1 km = 1000 m
650 m

3 km 400 m + 1 km 650 m = 3400 m + 1650 m
= 5050 m
= 5 km 50 m

5000 m = 5 km

The total distance of the race is 5 kilometers 50 meters.

b) How much further did Zoe have to cycle than run?

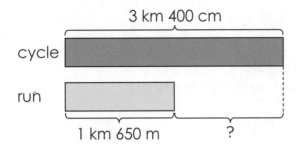

3 km 400 m − 1 km 650 m = ☐ km ☐ m

Method 1

First, subtract the kilometers. Then, subtract the meters.

$3 \text{ km } 400 \text{ m} \xrightarrow{-1 \text{ km}} 2 \text{ km } 400 \text{ m} \xrightarrow{-650 \text{ m}} ?$

$\underbrace{\text{1 km 1400 m}} \xrightarrow{-650 \text{ m}} 1 \text{ km } 750 \text{ m}$

(2 km 400 m) 1 km 1400 m

Method 2

3 km 400 m − 1 km 650 m = 3400 m − 1650 m

= ☐ m

= ☐ km ☐ m

Zoe had to cycle ☐ kilometer ☐ meters more than she ran.

Let's Do

1. Add or subtract.

a) 2 km 400 m + 265 m = _____ km _____ m

b) 4 km 850 m − 3 km 85 km = _____ km _____ m

c) 5 km 690 m + 520 m = _____ km _____ m

d) 9 km 420 m − 780 m = _____ km _____ m

e) 7 km 960 m + 2 km 240 m = _____ km _____ m

f) 8 km 30 m − 3 km 480 m = _____ km _____ m

P/B Chapter 8: Exercise 5, pages 16–19

Practice 2

1. Express in meters.

   a) 3 km

   b) 1 km 450 m

   c) 2 km 506 m

   d) 2 km 60 m

   e) 3 km 78 m

   f) 6 km 8 m

2. Express in kilometers and meters.

   a) 1680 m

   b) 1085 m

   c) 2204 m

   d) 3090 m

   e) 3999 m

   f) 4001 m

3. Arrange the distances in order. Begin with the longest.

   6007 m   6 km 770 m   6 km 70 m   6700 m

4. Subtract.

   a) 1 km – 800 m

   b) 1 km – 600 m

   c) 2 km – 1 km 45 m

   d) 1 km – 40 m

   e) 5 km – 4 km 940 m

   f) 2 km – 275 m

5. Add or subtract.

   a) 2 km 650 m + 3 km

   b) 3 km 460 m + 50 m

   c) 3 km 300 m + 800 m

   d) 4 km 700 m + 1 km 300 m

   e) 5 km 950 m – 4 km

   f) 4 km 820 m – 720 m

   g) 6 km 25 m – 3 km 350 m

   h) 5 km 40 m – 3 km 990 m

Lesson 3 Millimeters

You will learn to...
- measure and compare lengths in millimeters
- express centimeters and millimeters in millimeters
- express millimeters in centimeters and millimeters
- add and subtract lengths in centimeters and millimeters

Length in millimeters

Let's Learn

The **millimeter** is another unit of length.
We write **mm** for millimeter.

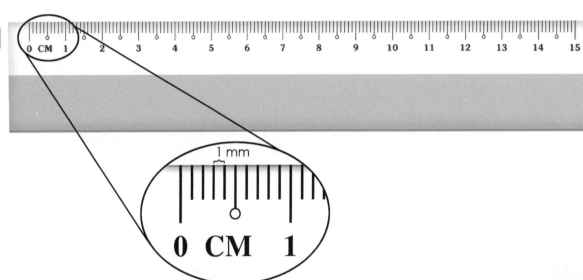

1 centimeter = 10 millimeters
1 cm = 10 mm

1 centimeter is 10 times
as long as 1 millimeter.

 We use millimeters to measure
the length of very short objects.

An ant is about 7 millimeters long.

1. Fill in the blanks with **millimeters**, **centimeters**, **meters** or **kilometers**.

   a) The length of my ruler is about 15 _____.

   b) The length of a paper clip is 30 _____.

   c) A basketball hoop is about 2 _____ tall.

   d) The distance from the swimming pool to the
   park is about 5 _____.

Expressing centimeters and millimeters in millimeters

Let's Learn

a) The thickness of the book is 1 centimeter 3 millimeters.
   What is the thickness in millimeters?

1 cm 3 mm

1 cm 3 mm ⟨ 1 cm = 10 mm
            3 mm

1 cm 3 mm = 10 mm + 3 mm
          = 13 mm

The thickness of the book is 13 millimeters.

b) What is 2 centimeters 8 millimeters in millimeters?

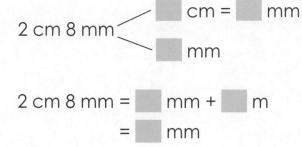

2 cm 8 mm ⟨ ▢ cm = ▢ mm
            ▢ mm

1 cm = 10 mm
2 cm = ▢ mm

2 cm 8 mm = ▢ mm + ▢ m
          = ▢ mm

1. Express in millimeters.

   a) 5 cm = _____ mm

   b) 6 cm 4 mm = _____ mm

   c) 7 cm 3 mm = _____ mm

   d) 8 cm 2 mm = _____ mm

Expressing millimeters in centimeters and millimeters

Let's Learn

a) A paper clip is 32 millimeters long.
   What is its length in centimeters and millimeters?

   32 mm ⟨ 30 mm = 3 cm
           2 mm

   10 mm = 1 cm

   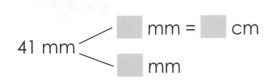

   32 mm = 3 cm + 2 mm
         = 3 cm 2 mm

   The length of the paper clip is 3 cm 2 mm.

b) What is 41 millimeters in centimeters and millimeters?

   41 mm ⟨ ▢ mm = ▢ cm
           ▢ mm

   41 mm = ▢ cm + ▢ mm
         = ▢ cm ▢ mm

Let's Do

1. Express in centimeters and millimeters.

   a) 60 mm = _____ cm

   b) 56 mm = _____ cm _____ mm

   c) 75 mm = _____ cm _____ mm

   d) 84 mm = _____ cm _____ mm

Comparing lengths in centimeters and millimeters

Let's Learn

The lengths of some objects are shown below.

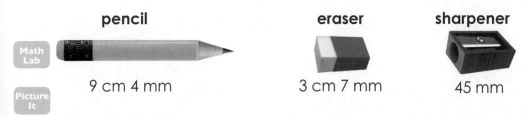

pencil
9 cm 4 mm

eraser
3 cm 7 mm

sharpener
45 mm

Which object is the shortest?

9 cm 4 mm = ☐ mm

3 cm 7 mm = ☐ mm

The ☐ is the shortest.

Let's Do

1. Arrange the lengths in order. Begin with the longest.

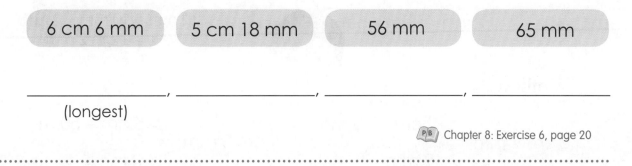

| 6 cm 6 mm | 5 cm 18 mm | 56 mm | 65 mm |

_____, _____, _____, _____
(longest)

PB Chapter 8: Exercise 6, page 20

Adding and subtracting centimeters and millimeters

 Let's Learn

Rosa has two magnets.
The red magnet is 2 centimeters 9 millimeters long.
The blue magnet is 5 centimeters 3 millimeters long.

a) What is the total length of Rosa's magnets?

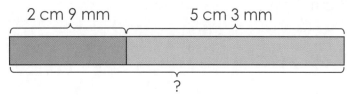

2 cm 9 mm + 5 cm 3 mm = ▨ cm ▨ mm

Method 1

First, add the centimeters.
Then, add the millimeters.

2 cm 9 mm $\xrightarrow{+ 5 \text{ cm}}$ 7 cm 9 mm $\xrightarrow{+ 3 \text{ mm}}$ 7 cm 12 mm = 8 cm 2 mm

12 mm = 10 mm + 2 mm
= 1 cm 2 mm

Method 2

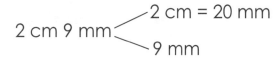

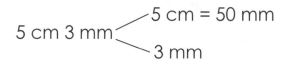

2 cm 9 mm + 5 cm 3 mm = 29 mm + 53 mm
= 82 mm
= ▨ cm ▨ mm

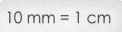 10 mm = 1 cm

The total length of Rosa's magnets is
▨ centimeters ▨ millimeters.

b) How much longer is the blue magnet than the red magnet?

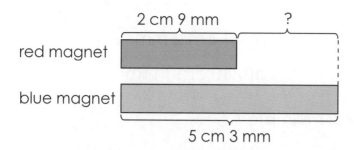

5 cm 3 mm − 2 cm 9 mm = ⬜ cm ⬜ mm

Method 1

First, subtract the centimeters. Then, subtract the millimeters.

5 cm 3 mm $\xrightarrow{-2\ cm}$ 3 cm 3 mm $\xrightarrow{-9\ mm}$?

2 cm 13 mm $\xrightarrow{-9\ mm}$ 2 cm 4 mm

Method 2

5 cm 3 mm − 2 cm 9 mm = 53 mm − 29 mm

= ⬜ mm

= ⬜ cm ⬜ mm

The blue magnet is ⬜ centimeters ⬜ millimeters longer than the red magnet.

Let's Do

1. Add or subtract.

   a) 3 cm 3 mm + 4 mm = _____ cm _____ mm

   b) 8 cm 9 mm − 1 cm 6 mm = _____ cm _____ mm

   c) 4 cm 9 mm + 2 cm 7 mm = _____ cm _____ mm

   d) 9 cm 2 mm − 5 cm 6 mm = _____ cm _____ mm

PB Chapter 8: Exercise 7, page 21

Practice 3

1. Express in millimeters.

   a) 2 cm

   b) 1 cm 2 mm

   c) 3 cm 4 mm

   d) 10 cm 1 mm

2. Express in centimeters and millimeters.

   a) 60 mm

   b) 48 mm

   c) 99 mm

   d) 109 mm

3. Arrange the lengths in order. Begin with the shortest.

   5 cm 5 mm   54 mm   4 cm 16 mm   48 mm

4. Add or subtract.

   a) 1 cm + 2 cm 2 mm

   b) 7 cm – 5 cm 1 mm

   c) 3 cm 7 mm + 6 cm 3 mm

   d) 10 cm 4 mm – 8 cm 9 mm

Lesson 4   Problem Solving

Word problems

Let's Learn

There are 4 roads in a town. Each road is 260 kilometers long.
What is the total length of the roads in the town?

1 Understand the problem.

How long is each road?
What do I have to find?

2 Plan what to do.

I can **draw a bar model**.

3 Work out the Answer.

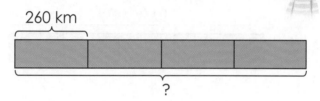

260 km × 4 = 1040 km
The total length of the roads in the town
is 1040 kilometers.

4 Check
Did you answer the question?
Is your answer correct?

1040 ÷ 4 = 260   ✓
My answer is correct.

- ☑ 1. Understand
- ☑ 2. Plan
- ☑ 3. Answer
- ☑ 4. Check

Let's Do

1. The lampposts along a street are placed 48 meters apart. What is the distance between the first lamppost and the sixth lamppost?

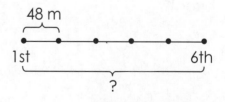

- ☐ 1. Understand
- ☐ 2. Plan
- ☐ 3. Answer
- ☐ 4. Check

The total length of a roll of red tape and 3 rolls of green tape is 9 meters 67 centimeters. If each roll of green tape is 2 meters long, what is the length of the roll of red tape?

1 Understand the problem.

How many rolls of tape are there?
How long is each roll of green tape?
What do I have to find?

2 Plan what to do.

I can **draw a bar model**.

3 Work out the **Answer**.

9 m 67 cm

?   2 m

$2 \text{ m} \times 3 = 6 \text{ m}$

The length of the 3 rolls of green tape is 6 meters.

9 m 67 cm – 6 m = ▢ m ▢ cm

The length of the roll of red tape is
▢ meters ▢ centimeters.

4 Check
Did you answer the question?
Is your answer correct?

6 m + ▢ m ▢ cm = 9 m 67 cm ✓

My answer is correct.

☑ 1. Understand
☑ 2. Plan
☑ 3. Answer
☑ 4. Check

1. Jane and 4 of her friends took part in a race.
   They ran a total distance of 2 kilometers 220 meters.
   Jane ran 1 kilometer 480 meters.
   If each of her 4 friends ran the same distance,
   how far did each friend run?

   > What is the total distance
   > Jane's 4 friends ran?

   ☐ 1. Understand
   ☐ 2. Plan
   ☐ 3. Answer
   ☐ 4. Check

P/B Chapter 8: Exercise 8, pages 22–25

Practice 4

Solve the word problems. Draw bar models to help you.
Show your work clearly.

1. A bean sprout was 2 centimeters 7 millimeters tall in the morning.
   It grew 1 centimeter 4 millimeters taller by the end of the day.
   How tall was the bean sprout at the end of the day?

2. Alice's towel was 30 centimeters long at first. It shrank
   1 centimeter 2 millimeters after washing. How long was Alice's
   towel after washing?

3. The distance around a running track is 400 meters. Anne ran
   round the track 6 times. What is the total distance she ran?
   Express your answer in kilometers and meters.

4. May has 112 meters of cloth. She made 4 similar dresses
   for her sisters. What is the length of the cloth she used to
   make each dress?

5. The total distance traveled by 2 trucks and a car is
   9 kilometers 670 meters. If the distance traveled by
   each truck is 4 kilometers, what is the distance
   traveled by the car?

6. Jack is 1 meter 32 centimeters tall. He is 43 centimeters shorter than his father. What is the total height of Jack and his father?

Mind stretcher

John's family went on a cross-country drive. The distance they traveled every day followed a pattern.

How many kilometers did they travel on Day 10?

| Day 1: 70 km |
| Day 2: 80 km |
| Day 3: 60 km |
| Day 4: 70 km |
| Day 5: 50 km |

1 **Understand** the problem.

Did they travel the same distance every day?
How many days are given?
What do I have to find?

2 **Plan** what to do.

I can **look for the pattern**.

3 Work out the **Answer**.

Day	1	2	3	4	5	6	7	8	9	10
Distance (km)	70	80	60	70	50					

+10 −20 +10 −20

They traveled ▢ kilometers on Day 10.

4 **Check**
Did you answer the question?
Is your answer correct?

By working backwards, I get 50 kilometers on Day 5.
My answer follows the pattern.
My answer is correct.

☑ 1. Understand
☑ 2. Plan
☑ 3. Answer
☑ 4. Check

Mass

1. The kilogram (kg) is a unit of mass.
   We use kilogram for heavy objects.

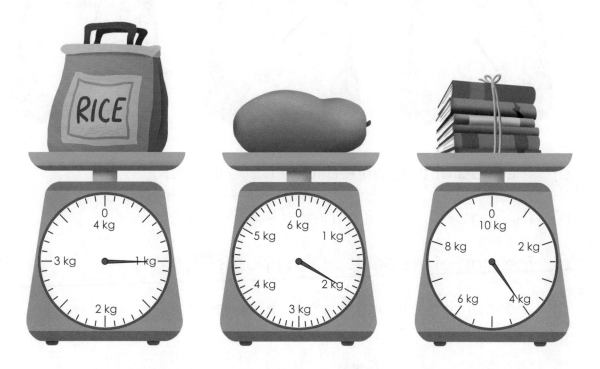

a) The mass of the sack of rice is 1 kilogram.

b) The mass of the pawpaw is more than 1 kilogram.

    It is ▮ kilograms.

c) The books are ▮ kilograms heavier than
    the pawpaw.

d) The sack of rice is ▮ kilograms lighter than
    the stack of books.

e) The ▮ is the lightest.

f) The ▮ is the heaviest.

35

2. The gram (g) is another unit of mass.
   We use gram for light objects.

a) The mass of the canned food is 300 grams.

b) The mass of the loaf of bread is ▢ grams.

c) The mass of the bottle of shampoo is ▢ grams.

d) The loaf of bread is ▢ grams heavier than
   the canned food.

e) The canned food is ▢ grams lighter than
   the bottle of shampoo.

f) Arrange the objects in order.
   Begin with the lightest.

   (lightest)

Lesson 1   Kilograms and Grams

You will learn to...
- measure and compare mass in kilograms and grams
- express kilograms and grams in grams
- express grams in kilograms and grams
- solve word problems on mass in kilograms and grams

Mass in kilograms and grams

Let's Learn

The kilogram (kg) and gram (g) are units of mass.

1 kilogram is 1000 times as heavy as 1 gram.

> 1 kilogram = 1000 g
> 1 kg = 1000 g

a)

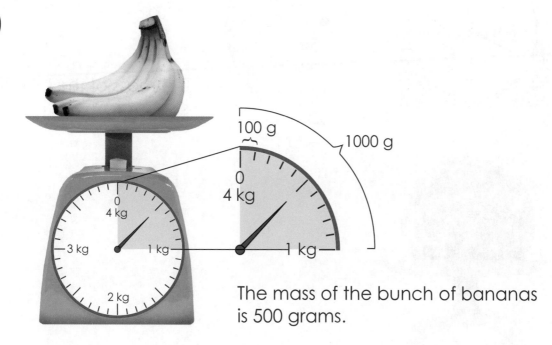

The mass of the bunch of bananas is 500 grams.

b)

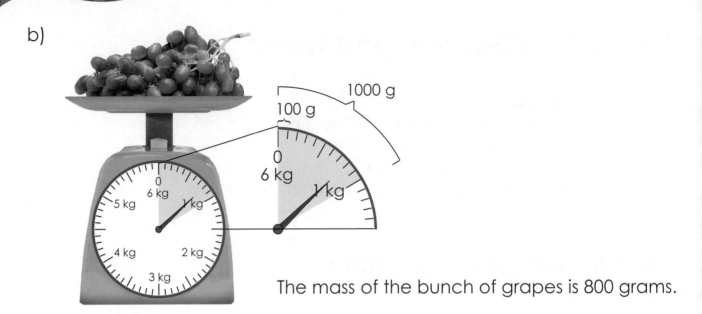

The mass of the bunch of grapes is 800 grams.

c)

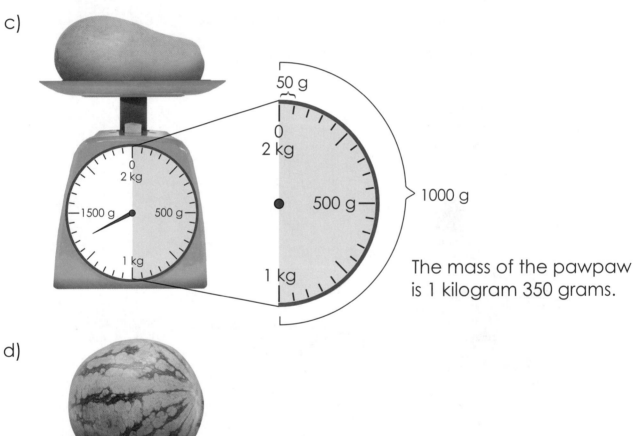

The mass of the pawpaw
is 1 kilogram 350 grams.

d)

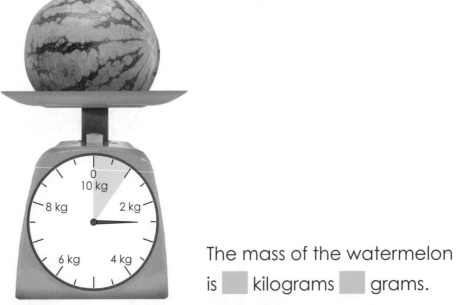

The mass of the watermelon

is ▢ kilograms ▢ grams.

1. Read the scales. Fill in the blanks.

a)

_____ kg

b)

_____ kg _____ g

c)

_____ kg _____ g

d)

_____ kg _____ g

e)

_____ kg _____ g

f)

_____ kg _____ g

P/B Chapter 9: Exercise 1, pages 26–27

Expressing kilograms and grams in grams

Let's Learn

a) The mass of a bag of potatoes is 2 kilograms 200 grams.
   What is the mass in grams?

   2 kg 200 g ⟨ 2 kg = 2000 g
                200 g

   1 kg = 1000 g

   2 kg 200 g = 2000 g + 200 g
              = 2200 g

   The mass of the bag of potatoes is 2200 grams.

b) What is 1 kilogram 400 grams in grams?

   1 kg 400 g ⟨ ▢ kg = ▢ g
                ▢ g

   1 kg 400 g = ▢ g + ▢ g
              = ▢ g

40

1. Express in grams.

   a)   3 kg = _____ g

   b)   4 kg 600 g = _____ g

   c)   5 kg 80 g = _____ g

   d)   6 kg 4 g = _____ g

Expressing grams in kilograms and grams

Let's Learn

a)   The mass of a bag of peanuts is 1850 grams.
     What is the mass in kilogram and grams?

$$1850\ g \begin{cases} 1000\ g = 1\ kg \\ 850\ g \end{cases}$$

1850 g = 1 kg + 850 g
       = 1 kg 850 g

The mass of the bag of peanuts is 1 kilogram 850 grams.

b)   What is 3080 g in kilograms and grams?

$$3080\ g \begin{cases} \boxed{}\ g = \boxed{}\ kg \\ \boxed{}\ g \end{cases}$$

1000 g = 1 kg
3000 g = 3 kg

3080 g = ☐ kg + ☐ g
       = ☐ kg ☐ g

1. Express in kilograms and grams.

    a) 1234 g = _____ kg _____ g

    b) 2340 g = _____ kg _____ g

    c) 3400 g = _____ kg _____ g

    d) 4050 g = _____ kg _____ g

P/B Chapter 9: Exercise 2, pages 28–30

Comparing mass in kilograms and grams

Let's Learn

The mass of the school bag is 3 kilograms 800 grams.

The mass of the bag of potatoes is 3 kilograms 600 grams.

The school bag is heavier than the bag of potatoes.

The bag of potatoes is ▢ than the school bag.

The mass of the sack of rice is ▢ kilograms ▢ grams.

The school bag is ▢ than the sack of rice.

Which object is the heaviest? ▢

Let's Do

1. Fill in the blanks.

2 kg 100 g   2090 g   1900 g   2 kg 10 g

a) The mass of the box of washing detergent is

_____ grams.

b) The mass of the bag of flour is _____ grams.

c) The box of washing detergent is _____ than the bottle of cooking oil.

d) The bottle of shampoo is _____ than the bag of flour.

e) Arrange the objects in order. Begin with the lightest.

_____, _____, _____, _____

(lightest)

2. Which is heavier, the fish or the chicken? _____

1100 g   1 kg 250 g

P/B Chapter 9: Exercise 3, page 31

Adding and subtracting kilograms and grams

Let's Learn

a) The mass of a watermelon is 3 kilograms 80 grams.
   The mass of a bunch of bananas is 1 kilogram 960 grams.
   What is their total mass?

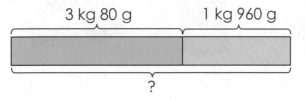

Picture It

3 kg 80 g + 1 kg 960 g = ☐ kg ☐ g

Method 1

3 kg 80 g $\xrightarrow{+1\,kg}$ 4 kg 80 g $\xrightarrow{+960\,g}$ 4 kg 1040 g = 5 kg 40 g

1040 g = 1000 g + 40 g

Method 2

3 kg 80 g ⟨ 3 kg = 3000 g
            80 g

1 kg 960 g ⟨ 1 kg = 1000 g
             960 g

3 kg 80 g + 1 kg 960 g = 3080 g + 1960 g
                       = 5040 g
                       = 5 kg 40 g

5040 g = 5000 g + 40 g

Their total mass is 5 kilograms 40 grams.

b) The mass of a bottle filled with marbles is 3 kilograms 400 grams.
The mass of the empty bottle is 1 kilogram 450 grams.
What is the mass of the marbles?

3 kg 400 g   1 kg 450 g

Total mass of bottle and marbles = mass of empty bottle + mass of marbles

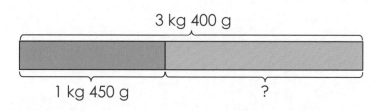

3 kg 400 g – 1 kg 450 g = ▢ kg ▢ g

Method 1

3 kg 400 g $\xrightarrow{-1\text{ kg}}$ 2 kg 400 g $\xrightarrow{-450\text{ g}}$?

1 kg 1400 g $\xrightarrow{-450\text{ g}}$ 1 kg 950 g

First, subtract the kilograms.
Then, subtract the grams.

Method 2

3 kg 400 g = ▢ g   1 kg 450 g = ▢ g

3 kg 400 g – 1 kg 450 g = ▢ g – ▢ g

= ▢ g

= ▢ kg ▢ g

The mass of the marbles is ▢ kilogram ▢ grams.

1. Add or subtract.

   a) 2 kg 940 g + 300 g = _____ kg _____ g

   b) 3 kg 880 g + 1 kg 220 g = _____ kg _____ g

   c) 4 kg – 1 kg 480 g = _____ kg _____ g

   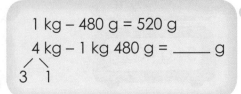

   1 kg – 480 g = 520 g

   4 kg – 1 kg 480 g = _____ g
          3   1

   d) 5 kg 20 g – 2 kg 450 g = _____ kg _____ g

P/B Chapter 9: Exercise 4, pages 32–35

Practice 1

1. Express in grams.

   a) 1 kg 456 g   b) 2 kg 370 g   c) 3 kg 808 g
   d) 2 kg 80 g   e) 1 kg 8 g   f) 4 kg 7 g

2. Express in kilograms and grams.

   a) 2143 g   b) 1354 g   c) 3800 g
   d) 2206 g   e) 3085 g   f) 4009 g

3. Subtract.

   a) 1 kg – 395 g   b) 1 kg – 85 g   c) 3 kg – 2 kg 400 g
   d) 5 kg – 4 kg 60 g   e) 1 kg – 540 g   f) 3 kg – 805 g

4. Add or subtract.

   a) 3 kg 500 g + 2 kg   b) 4 kg 650 g + 450 g
   c) 3 kg 100 g + 1 kg 900 g   d) 2 kg 50 g + 4 kg 70 g
   e) 3 kg 10 g – 200 g   f) 4 kg 300 g – 1 kg 50 g
   g) 4 kg 250 g – 1 kg 500 g   h) 5 kg – 2 kg 905 g

5. Look at the scales and answer the questions.
   Express your answers in kilograms and grams.

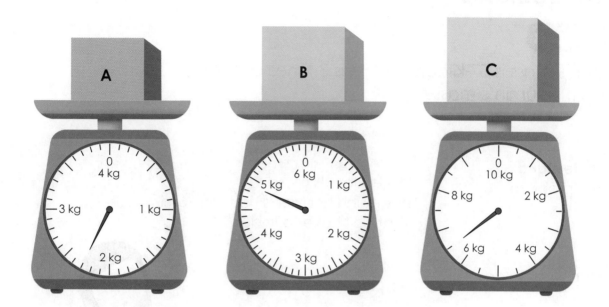

a) What is the mass of Box A?
b) How much heavier is Box B than Box A?
c) How much lighter is Box B than Box C?

6. What is the mass of the bag of peanuts?
   How much more peanuts are needed to
   obtain 2 kilograms?

Lesson 2 Problem Solving

Word problems

Let's Learn

Jack's mass is 57 kilograms. He is 3 times as heavy as Sumin.
What is Sumin's mass?

1 **Understand** the problem.

What is Jack's mass?
How much heavier is he than Sumin?
What do I have to find?

2 **Plan** what to do.

I can **draw a bar model**.

3 Work out the **Answer**.

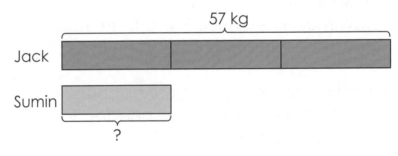

57 kg

Jack

Sumin

?

$57 \div 3 = 19$
Sumin's mass is 19 kilograms.

4 **Check**
Did you answer the question?
Is your answer correct?

$3 \times 19 = 57$ ✓
My answer is correct.

☑ 1. Understand
☑ 2. Plan
☑ 3. Answer
☑ 4. Check

48

1. A watermelon is 5 times as heavy as a pawpaw. If the mass of the pawpaw is 950 grams, what is the mass of the watermelon?

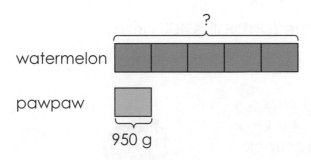

□ 1. Understand
□ 2. Plan
□ 3. Answer
□ 4. Check

The total mass of a football and 10 tennis balls is 1 kilogram. If the mass of each tennis ball is 60 grams, what is the mass of the football?

1 **Understand** the problem.

What is the total mass of the football and tennis balls?
What is the mass of one tennis ball?
What do I have to find?

2 **Plan** what to do.

I can draw a bar model to help me find the answer. First, I have to find the total mass of the 10 tennis balls.

3 Work out the **Answer**.

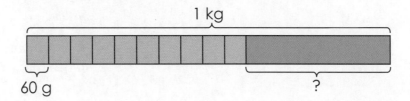

$60 \text{ g} \times 10 = 600 \text{ g}$

The mass of 10 tennis balls is 600 grams.

$$1 \text{ kg} - 600 \text{ g} = 1000 \text{ g} - 600 \text{ g}$$
$$= 400 \text{ g}$$

The mass of the football is 400 grams.

 Check
Did you answer the question? Is your answer correct?

$$400 \text{ g} + 600 \text{ g} = 1000 \text{ g}$$
$$= 1 \text{ kg} ✓$$
My answer is correct.

☑ 1. Understand
☑ 2. Plan
☑ 3. Answer
☑ 4. Check

Let's Do

1. The total mass of a tin of cooking oil and 2 bags of sugar is 5 kilograms 50 grams. If the mass of each bag of sugar is 2 kilograms, what is the mass of the tin of cooking oil?

What is the mass of 2 bags of sugar?

☐ 1. Understand
☐ 2. Plan
☐ 3. Answer
☐ 4. Check

Chapter 9: Exercise 5, pages 36–39

Practice 2

Solve the word problems. Draw bar models to help you.
Show your work clearly.

1. Ryan's mass is 14 kilograms.
   His father is 6 times as heavy as he is.
   Find his father's mass.

2. Lily's mass was 25 kilograms 750 grams two years ago.
   Now her mass is 32 kilograms.
   How much heavier is Lily now than two years ago?

3. A basket of fruits has a mass of 1 kilogram 60 grams.
   The empty basket has a mass of 200 grams.
   Find the mass of the fruits.

4. A jackfruit has a mass of 2 kilograms 990 grams.
   A watermelon has a mass of 4 kilograms 200 grams.

   a) Find the total mass of the two fruits.
   b) Find the difference in mass between the two fruits.

5. A watermelon has a mass of 2 kilograms 50 grams.
   A pumpkin is 600 grams heavier than the watermelon.

   a) What is the mass of the pumpkin?
   b) What is the total mass of the watermelon and
      the pumpkin?

6. The total mass of an apple and 2 pears is 330 grams.
   The mass of the apple is 90 grams. If the pears have the
   same mass, what is the mass of each pear?

7. David's mass is 39 kilograms.
   Hassan is twice as heavy as David.
   Mingli's mass is 27 kilograms less than Hassan's.
   What is Mingli's mass?

Mind stretcher

Let's Learn

A year ago, Ken and Gerald had a total mass of 120 kilograms. Then, Ken's mass increased by 2 kilograms and Gerald's mass went down by 2 kilograms. Now, they both have the same mass. Find the mass of each boy one year ago.

1 **Understand** the problem.

> How many people are there?
> Do they have the same mass?
> How many kilograms did Ken put on?
> How many kilograms did Gerald lose?
> What do I need to find?

2 **Plan** what to do.

> I can **draw a bar model** and **work backwards**.

3 Work out the **Answer**.

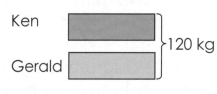 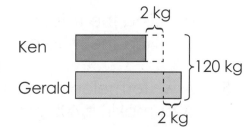

Total mass = 120 + 2 – 2
= 120 kg

> The total mass is still the same.

120 ÷ 2 = 60
The mass of each boy now is 60 kilograms.

60 – 2 = 58
One year ago, Ken's mass was 58 kilograms.

60 + 2 = 62
One year ago, Gerald's mass was 62 kilograms.

4 **Check**
Did you answer the question? Is your answer correct?

> 58 + 62 = 120 ✓
> My answer is correct.

☑ 1. Understand
☑ 2. Plan
☑ 3. Answer
☑ 4. Check

P/B Review 4, pages 40–48

Volume and Capacity

1.

The mass of the watermelon is [ ] g.

2.

The mass of the bag is 3 kg [ ] g.

3. 1 kg = 1000 g

2 kg = [ ] g
4 kg = [ ] g

4. What is 1 kilogram 680 grams in grams?

1 kg 680 g
        1 kg = [ ] g
        [ ] g

1 kg 680 g = [ ] g + [ ] g
          = [ ] g

1 kilogram 680 grams is 680 grams more than 1 kg.

5. What is 2750 grams in kilograms and grams?

2750 g ⟨ ▢ g = ▢ kg
       750 g

▢ 1000 g = 1 kg

2750 g = ▢ kg ▢ g

6. a) 3 kg 470 g + 1 kg 280 g = 4 kg ▢ g

First, add the kilograms. Then, add the grams.

   b) 2 kg 850 g + 4 kg 693 g = ▢ kg ▢ g

2 kg 850 g ——+ 4 kg——▶ 6 kg 850 g ——+ 693 g——▶ 6 kg 1543 g = ▢ kg ▢ g

2 kg 850 g = 2850 g
4 kg 693 g = 4693 g
2850 g + 4693 g = ▢ g

7. a) 5 kg 960 g – 2 kg 340 g = 3 kg ▢ g

First, subtract the kilograms. Then, subtract the grams.

   b) 3 kg 280 g – 1 kg 470 g = ▢ kg ▢ g

3 kg 280 g ——– 1 kg——▶ 1 kg 1280 g ——– 470 g——▶ = ▢ kg ▢ g

3 kg 280 g = 3280 g
1 kg 470 g = 1470 g
3280 g – 1470 g = ▢ g

Lesson 1   Volume

You will learn to...
- compare the volume of liquid in two or more containers

Understanding volume

Let's Learn

Glass A, Glass B and Glass C are identical.

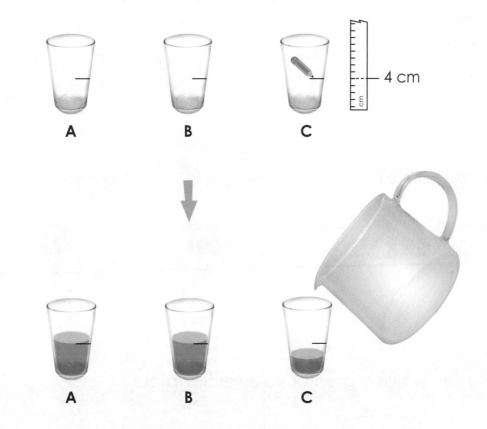

Math Lab

Picture It

4 cm

Glass A and Glass B contain the same amount of liquid.
They have the same **volume** of liquid.

Glass C contains less liquid than Glass A and Glass B.
The volume of liquid in Glass C is less than the volume of
liquid in Glass A and Glass B.

The volume of a liquid is the amount of space it takes up.

Pour all the liquid from Glass A
into Container D.

Pour all the liquid from Glass B
into Container E.

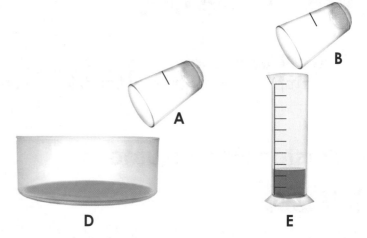

Which contains a greater
volume of liquid,
Container D or Container E?

Pour the liquid back
into the glasses.

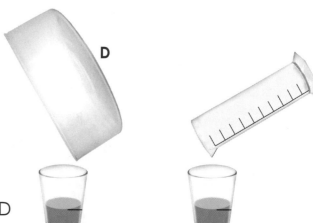

What do you notice?

The volume of liquid in Container D
and Container E is [ ].

 **Think About It**

Which container has a greater volume of water?

Both containers have
the same level of water.
So, they contain the
same volume of water.

Yen

Is Yen correct? Explain why.

Comparing volumes

There is some strawberry milk in each of these bottles.

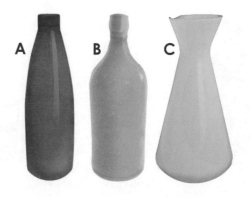

All the milk in each bottle is poured into identical glasses.

Bottle A contains 3 glasses of milk.

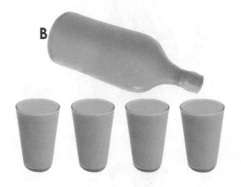

Bottle B contains 4 glasses of milk.

Bottle C contains 2 glasses of milk.

The volume of milk in Bottle A is less than the volume of milk in Bottle B.

The volume of milk in Bottle A is ▢ the volume of milk in Bottle C.

Bottle B contains the greatest volume of milk.
Bottle ▢ contains the smallest volume of milk.

Bottle A fills fewer glasses than Bottle B.

1. All the juice in each jug is poured into identical glasses.

Fill in the blanks.

a) Jug _____ contains more juice than Jug A.

b) Jug _____ contains less juice than Jug A.

c) Jug _____ contains the smallest volume of juice.

d) Jug _____ contains the greatest volume of juice.

P/B Chapter 10: Exercise 1, pages 49–51

Practice 1

1. Look at the containers below and answer the questions.

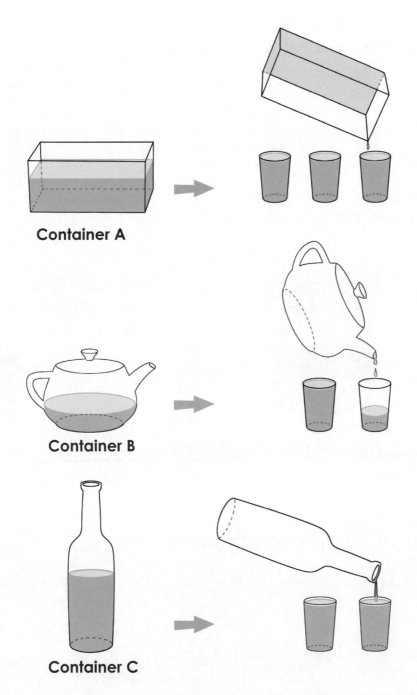

Container A

Container B

Container C

a) Which container holds more liquid than Container C?

b) Which container holds a greater volume of liquid than Container C?

c) Which container holds the least amount of liquid?

d) Which container holds the smallest volume of liquid?

Lesson 2   Liters

You will learn ...
- to measure and compare volume in liters
- the difference between volume and capacity

Volume in liters

Let's Learn

a)   Get a 1-liter beaker and find out
     how much 1 liter of water is.

This beaker is used
to measure the
volume of liquids.

We can measure the volume of liquids in **liters**.
We write **L** for liters.

b)   Get some paper cups.
     Find out how many paper cups you can fill with
     1 liter of juice.

Comparing volume in liters

The bottle contains 1 liter of water.

The glass contains less than 1 liter of water.

The jug contains more than 1 liter of water.

Let's Do

1. Look at the containers above and answer the questions.

   a) Which container holds the greatest volume
   of water? _____

   b) Which container holds the smallest volume
   of water? _____

 Chapter 10: Exercise 2, page 52

Volume and capacity

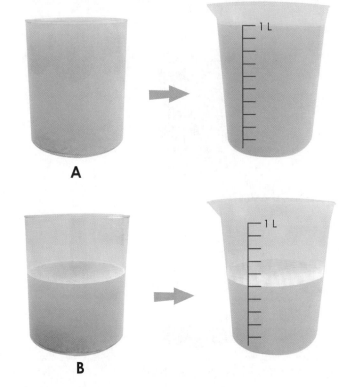

A

B

Jar A and Jar B are identical containers.
They can each hold 1 liter of liquid when full.
The **capacity** of each jar is 1 liter.

The capacity of a container is the amount it can hold when full.

There is less than 1 liter of liquid in Jar B.
The volume of liquid in Jar B is less than 1 liter.

The volume of liquid is the amount of liquid in the container.

Let's Do

1. Fill in the blanks with **capacity** or **volume**.

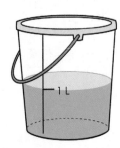

a) The _____ of the pail is 2 liters.

b) The _____ of water in the pail is 1 liter.

Comparing capacity

There is water left in the jug.

The jug can hold more water than the bottle.

The jug is not filled completely.

The bottle can hold less water than the jug.
The jug has a greater capacity than the bottle.

The jug and the basin can hold the same amount of water.
The jug and the basin have the same capacity.

Comparing capacity in liters

Let's Learn

All the water in the containers is poured into 1-liter beakers.

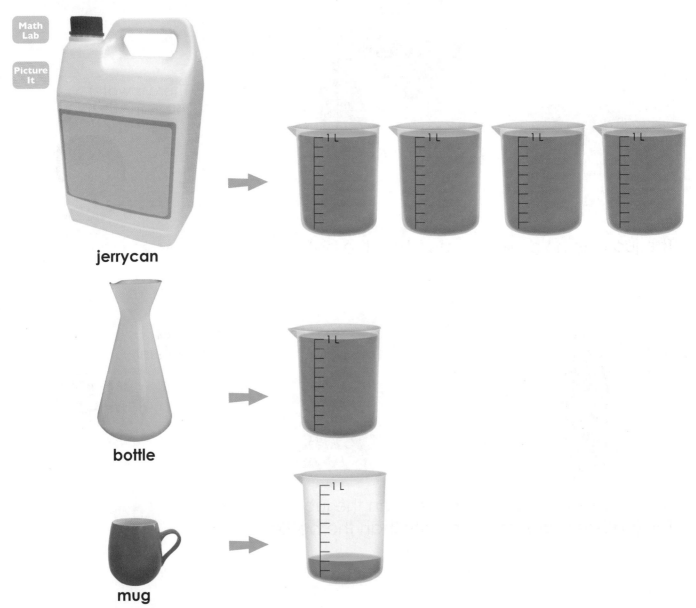

jerrycan

bottle

mug

The jerrycan can hold more than 1 liter of water.
The bottle can hold 1 liter of water.
The mug can hold less than 1 liter of water.

The capacity of the jerrycan is 4 liters.
The capacity of the bottle is 1 liter.

4 L – 1 L = ▮ L

The bottle can hold ▮ liters less than the jerrycan.

Let's Do

1. Look at the containers on page 64 and fill in the blanks.

   a) The _____ has the greatest capacity.

   b) The _____ has the smallest capacity.

2. a) Which of the following containers have a capacity of 1 liter, less than 1 liter or more than 1 liter?

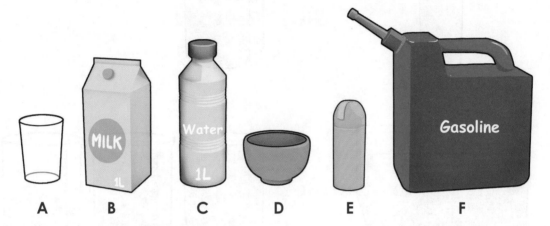

Capacity	Containers
1 liter	
less than 1 liter	
more than 1 liter	

   b) Get a container which you think can hold less than 1 liter of water. Fill it completely with water and then measure its capacity. Is it less than 1 liter? _____

   c) Get a container which you think can hold more than 1 liter of water. Fill it completely with water and then measure its capacity. Is it more than 1 liter? _____

3. Pail A can hold 12 liters of water.
   Pail B can hold 8 liters of water.

   a) Pail ____ has a greater capacity than Pail ____.

   b) It can hold ____ liters more water.

PB Chapter 10: Exercises 3–5, pages 53–56

Practice 2

1. All the water in the containers is poured into 1-liter beakers. Answer the questions.

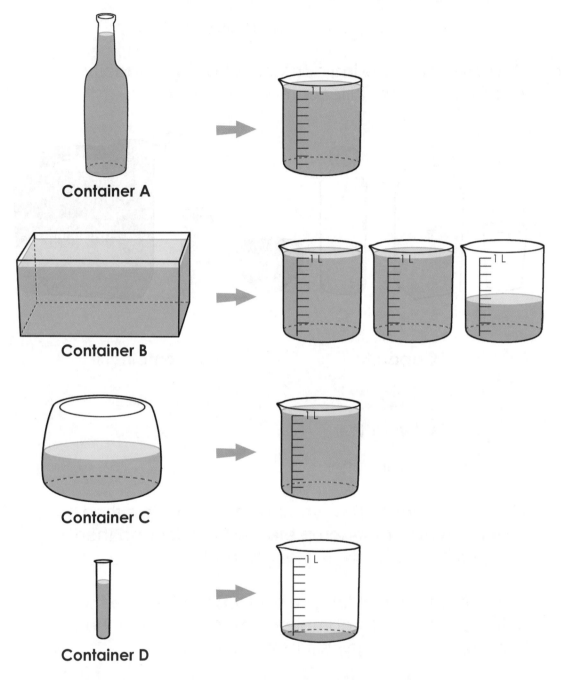

Container A

Container B

Container C

Container D

a) Does Container B contain more than or less than 1 liter of water?

b) Does Container D contain more than or less than 1 liter of water?

c) Which containers hold the same volume of water?

d) Which container holds the greatest volume of water?

e) Which container holds the smallest volume of water?

2.

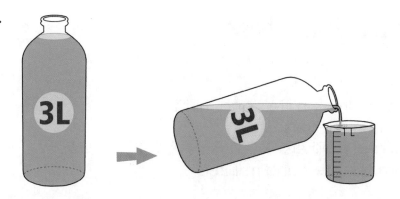

a) What is the capacity of the bottle?

b) After filling up a 1-liter beaker, what is the volume of water left in the bottle?

3.

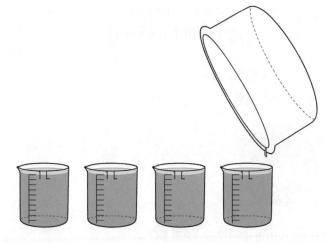

a) How many liters of water can the tub hold?
   What is the capacity of the tub?

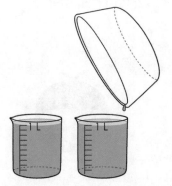

b) How many liters of water can the basin hold?
   What is the capacity of the basin?

c) Which container has a smaller capacity, the tub or the basin?

d) How much less water can it hold?

Lesson 3 Liters and Milliliters

You will learn to...
- measure and compare volumes in liters and milliliters
- express liters and milliliters in milliliters
- express milliliters in liters and milliliters
- add and subtract volumes in liters and milliliters

Liters and milliliters

Let's Learn

Math Lab

Picture It

a)

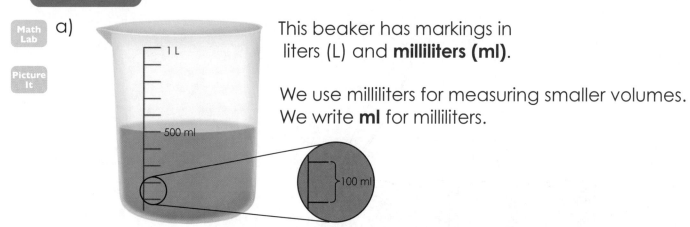

This beaker has markings in liters (L) and **milliliters (ml)**.

We use milliliters for measuring smaller volumes. We write **ml** for milliliters.

There is less than 1 liter of liquid in the beaker.
There are 500 milliliters of liquid in the beaker.
The volume of liquid in the beaker is 500 milliliters.
We can measure volume of liquids in liters and milliliters.

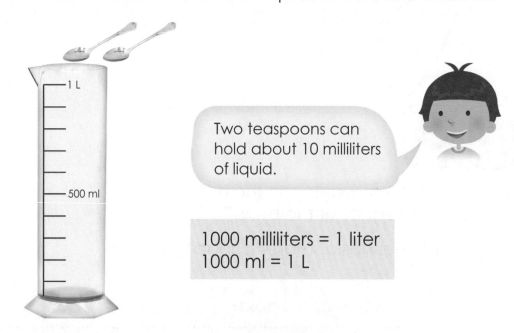

Two teaspoons can hold about 10 milliliters of liquid.

1000 milliliters = 1 liter
1000 ml = 1 L

b)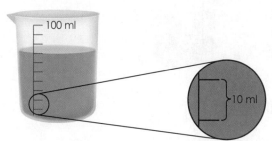

This is a 500-milliliter beaker.
The volume of liquid in the beaker
is 250 milliliters.

This is a 100-milliliter beaker.
The volume of liquid in the beaker
is ▢ milliliters.

Let's Do

1. What is the total volume of water in the beakers?

a)

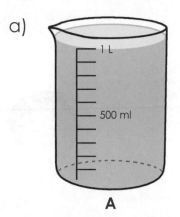  

A + B + C

= _____ L _____ ml

1 L, 1 L 500 ml,
1 L 600 ml

b)

 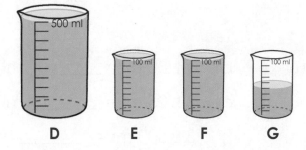

D + E + F + G

= _____ ml

P/B Chapter 10: Exercises 6–7, pages 57–62

Expressing liters and milliliters in milliliters

Let's Learn

Picture It a)

What is 2 liters 350 milliliters in milliliters?

2 L 350 ml 〈 2 L = 2000 ml
                350 ml

1 L = 1000 ml

2 L 350 ml = 2000 ml + 350 ml
           = 2350 ml

2 L 350 ml is 350 ml more than 2 L.

b) What is 3 liters 50 milliliters in milliliters?

3 L 50 ml 〈 ▢ L = ▢ ml
              ▢ ml

1 L = 1000 ml
3 L = ▢ ml

3 L 50 ml = ▢ ml + ▢ ml
          = ▢ ml

Let's Do

1. Write in milliliters.

a) 1 L 800 ml = _____ ml

b) 1 L 80 ml = _____ ml

c) 1 L 8 ml = _____ ml

d) 3 L 25 ml = _____ ml

e) 2 L 5 ml = _____ ml

f) 3 L 500 ml = _____ ml

Expressing milliliters in liters and milliliters

Let's Learn

Math Lab

a) Find the total amount of water in the two measuring beakers.

Picture It

1·4 3+

700 ml + 400 ml = 1100 ml

What is 1100 milliliters in liters and milliliters?

1100 ml ⟨ 1000 ml = 1 L
          100 ml

1100 ml = 1 L + 100 ml
        = 1 L 100 ml

b) What is 2050 milliliters in liters and milliliters?

2050 ml ⟨ ▢ ml = ▢ L
           ▢ ml

2050 ml = ▢ L + ▢ ml
        = ▢ L ▢ ml

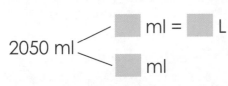

1. Express in liters and milliliters.

   a) 1200 ml = ____ L ____ ml   b) 2500 ml = ____ L ____ ml

   c) 2050 ml = ____ L ____ ml   d) 1005 ml = ____ L ____ ml

   e) 3400 ml = ____ L ____ ml   f) 3105 ml = ____ L ____ ml

Comparing in liters and milliliters

The beakers show the amount of liquid in each container.

 a)

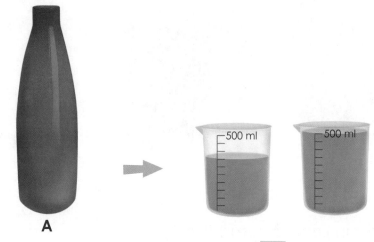

A

The capacity of Container A is ▢ milliliters.

350 + 500
= 35 tens + 50 tens
= 85 tens
= 850

b)

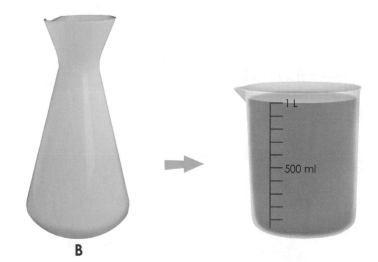

B

The capacity of Container B is ▢ milliliters.

c)

C

The capacity of Container C is ⬜ liter ⬜ milliliters.

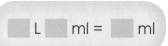
⬜ L ⬜ ml = ⬜ ml

d) The capacity of Container B is greater than the capacity of Container A.

e) The capacity of Container C is ⬜ the capacity of Container A.

Let's Do

1. Look at Container A, Container B and Container C. Arrange the containers in order. Begin with the container with the greatest capacity.

_____, _____, _____
(greatest)

P/B Chapter 10: Exercise 8, pages 63–64

Adding and subtracting liters and milliliters

Let's Learn

1 L 800 ml
A

3 L 350 ml
B

a) Find the total volume of liquid in the two containers.

1 L 800 ml + 3 L 350 ml = ▢ L ▢ ml

> First, add the liters.
> Then, add the milliliters.

Method 1

1 L 800 ml $\xrightarrow{+3 L}$ 4 L 800 ml $\xrightarrow{+350 ml}$ 4 L 1150 ml = 5 L 150 ml

> 1150 ml = 1000 ml + 150 ml

Method 2

1 L 800 ml ⟨ 1 L = 1000 ml / 800 ml

3 L 350 ml ⟨ 3 L = 3000 ml / 350 ml

1 L 800 ml + 3 L 350 ml = 1800 ml + 3350 ml
= 5150 ml
= 5 L 150 ml

The total volume of liquid in the two containers is
5 liters 150 milliliters.

b) Find the difference in the volume of liquid between the two containers.

3 L 350 ml – 1 L 800 ml = ☐ L ☐ ml

Method 1

First, subtract the liters.
Then, subtract the milliliters.

3 L 350 ml $\xrightarrow{-1\ L}$ 2 L 350 ml $\xrightarrow{-800\ ml}$?

1 L 1350 ml $\xrightarrow{-800\ ml}$ 1 L 550 ml

Method 2

3 L 350 ml – 1 L 800 ml = 3350 ml – 1800 ml
= ☐ ml
= ☐ L ☐ ml

The difference in the volume of liquid between the two containers is 1 liter 550 milliliters.

Let's Do

1. Add or subtract.

   a) 2 L + 4 L 750 ml = _____ L _____ ml

   b) 5 L 900 ml – 2 L 650 ml = _____ L _____ ml

   c) 1 L 450 ml + 3 L 550 ml = _____ L _____ ml

   d) 9 L 20 ml – 7 L 200 ml = _____ L _____ ml

2.

   How many more milliliters of water are needed to

   make up 2 liters? _____ ml

 Chapter 10: Exercises 9–10, pages 65–69

Practice 3

1. What is the total volume of water in the beakers?

2. Express in milliliters.

   a) 3 L
   b) 1 L 200 ml
   c) 2 L 55 ml
   d) 2 L 650 ml
   e) 3 L 65 ml
   f) 4 L 5 ml

3. Write in liters and milliliters.

   a) 5000 ml
   b) 1600 ml
   c) 2250 ml
   d) 3205 ml
   e) 2074 ml
   f) 1009 ml

4. Circle the correct answer.

   a) 1 L is more than / equal to / less than 980 ml.
   b) 2 L 50 ml is more than / equal to / less than 2050 ml.
   c) 4 L 8 ml is more than / equal to / less than 4800 ml.

5. Add or subtract.

   a) 1 L 500 ml + 500 ml
   b) 2 L 800 ml + 1 L 200 ml
   c) 3 L 300 ml + 750 ml
   d) 5 L 900 ml + 3 L 240 ml
   e) 2 L 800 ml – 1 L 780 ml
   f) 4 L – 1 L 850 ml
   g) 4 L 80 ml – 1 L 360 ml
   h) 6 L 5 ml – 2 L 80 ml

6.

   2 L 375 ml   1 L 750 ml   1755 ml   2150 ml
       A   B   C   D

   a) Which bottle contains the greatest volume of water?
   b) Which bottle contains the smallest volume of water?
   c) What is the total volume of water in the four bottles?

Lesson 4 Problem Solving

Word problems

Let's Learn

The capacity of a tank is 8 liters.
It contains 4 liters 650 milliliters of water.
How much more water is needed to fill up the tank completely?

1 **Understand** the problem.

> What does capacity mean?
> How many liters of water are in the tank?
> What do I have to find?

2 **Plan** what to do.

> I can **draw a bar model**.

3 Work out the **Answer**.

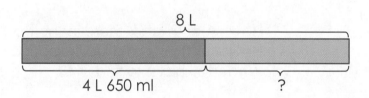

8 L

4 L 650 ml   ?

8 L − 4 L 650 ml = ☐ L ☐ ml

☐ liters ☐ milliliters more water is needed
to fill up the tank completely.

4 **Check**
Did you answer the question?
Is your answer correct?

> 4 L 650 ml + ☐ L ☐ ml = 8 L ✓
> My answer is correct.

☑ 1. Understand
☑ 2. Plan
☑ 3. Answer
☑ 4. Check

1. There are 96 liters of water in a tank.
74 liters of water are needed to fill up the tank completely.
What is the capacity of the tank?

I can draw a bar model.

☐ 1. Understand
☐ 2. Plan
☐ 3. Answer
☐ 4. Check

Let's Learn

A bottle contained 1 liter 46 milliliters of juice at first. David poured out the juice to fill 5 cups, each having a capacity of 150 milliliters. What volume of juice is left in the bottle?

1 **Understand** the problem.

How much juice is there in the bottle?
How much juice did David pour out?
What do I have to find first?

2 **Plan** what to do.

First, I have to find the amount of juice David poured out.

3 Work out the **Answer**.

150 ml × 5 = 750 ml
David poured out 750 milliliters of juice into the 5 cups.

1 L 46 ml − 750 ml = ▮ ml

▮ milliliters of juice are left in the bottle.

4 **Check**
Did you answer the question?
Is your answer correct?

▮ ml + 750 ml = 1 L 46 ml ✓
My answer is correct.

☑ 1. Understand
☑ 2. Plan
☑ 3. Answer
☑ 4. Check

1. There are 850 milliliters of water left in a bottle after Sally and her 3 friends drank some of it.
Each of them drank 220 milliliters of water.
How much water was there in the bottle at first?

_____ ◯ _____ = _____

They drank _____ milliliters of water altogether.

_____ ◯ _____ = _____

There were _____ milliliters of water in the bottle at first.

☐ 1. Understand
☐ 2. Plan
☐ 3. Answer
☐ 4. Check

P/B Chapter 10: Exercise 11, pages 70–73

Practice 4

Solve the word problems. Draw bar models to help you.
Show your work clearly.

1. Sally bought 10 packets of milk. Each packet contained 125 milliliters of milk. Find the total amount of milk in liters and milliliters.

2. The capacity of a container is 24 liters. How many pails of water are needed to fill the container completely if the capacity of the pail is 3 liters?

3. May pours 9 bottles of orange juice into a container and fills the container completely. Each bottle contains 2 liters of orange juice. What is the capacity of the container?

4. The capacity of Container A is 2 L 650 ml. The capacity of Container B is 5 L 300 ml.

   a) What is the total capacity of the two containers?
   b) How much more water can Container B hold than Container A?

5. Mr. Roberts bought 6 tins of paint. Each tin contained 3 liters of paint. He had 2 L 400 ml of paint left after painting his house. How much paint did he use?

6. There are 840 milliliters of water left in a bottle after Fred
    and his 3 friends shared some water equally.
    If the bottle contained 1 liter 800 milliliters of water at first,
    how many liters of water did each of them drink?

Write a word problem using these words and measurements.

jug	1 L 350 ml	more
3 L 745 ml	bottle	capacity

Mind stretcher

Let's Learn

Tank A and Tank B contain a total of 38 liters of water.
9 liters of water are poured from Tank A into Tank B.
Then, 8 liters of water are poured from Tank B into Tank A.
There is now an equal amount of water in both the tanks.
How much water was there in each tank at first?

1 Understand the problem.

How many tanks are there?
What is the total amount of water?
How much water is poured from Tank A into Tank B?
How much water is poured from Tank B into Tank A?
What do I need to find?

2 Plan what to do.

I can **work backwards**.
I start by finding the amount of
water in each tank in the end.

3 Work out the Answer.

Step 1:

38 L ÷ 2 = 19 L

There were 19 liters of water in each tank in the end.

Tank A | 19 L

Tank B | 19 L

Step 2:

Find the volume of water in each tank before pouring 8 liters of water from Tank B into Tank A.

Tank A | 11 L | 8 L   19 L – 8 L = 11 L

Tank B | 19 L | 8 L   19 L + 8 L = 27 L

Step 3:

Find the volume of water in each tank before pouring 9 liters of water from Tank A into Tank B.

Tank A | 11 L | 9 L   11 L + 9 L = 20 L

Tank B | 18 L | 9 L   27 L – 9 L = 18 L

Tank A had 20 liters of water and Tank B had 18 liters of water at first.

4 Check

Did you answer the question? Is your answer correct?

9 liters of water were poured from Tank A into Tank B.
Tank A: 20 L – 9 L = 11 L
Tank B: 18 L + 9 L = 27 L

Then, 8 liters of water were poured from Tank B into Tank A.
Tank A: 11 L + 8 L = 19 L
Tank B: 27 L – 8 L = 19 L

There is an equal amount of 19 liters of water in each tank in the end.
My answer is correct.

☑ 1. Understand
☑ 2. Plan
☑ 3. Answer
☑ 4. Check

Fractions

1. The circle is divided into 2 equal parts.

   Each part is a half $\left(\dfrac{1}{2}\right)$ of the circle.

   ▢ halves make a whole.

2. Each circle is divided into equal parts.

Fraction		Read as
	$\dfrac{1}{2}$	one-half
	$\dfrac{1}{3}$	one-third
	$\dfrac{1}{4}$	one-quarter or one-fourth
	$\dfrac{2}{5}$	two-fifths
	$\dfrac{5}{6}$	five-sixths
	$\dfrac{4}{7}$	four-sevenths

Fraction		Read as
	▢	three-eighths
	▢	two-ninths
	▢	seven-tenths
	▢	five-elevenths
	▢	one-twelfth

3.

2 out of 5 equal parts are shaded.

$\frac{2}{5}$ of the bar is shaded.

3 out of 5 equal parts are not shaded.

[ ] of the bar is not shaded.

[ ] and [ ] together make 1 whole.

1 whole = [ ] fifths

$1 = \dfrac{[\ ]}{5}$

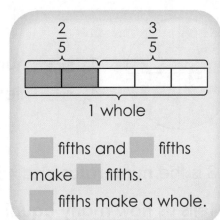

$\frac{2}{5}$ $\frac{3}{5}$

1 whole

[ ] fifths and [ ] fifths make [ ] fifths.

[ ] fifths make a whole.

4. The circles are of the same size.

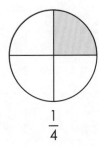

$\frac{1}{4}$

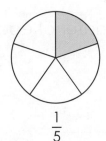

$\frac{1}{5}$

[ ] is greater than [ ].

Lesson 1   Fraction of a Whole

You will learn to...
- name parts of a fraction
- compare fractions

Naming parts of a fraction

Let's Learn

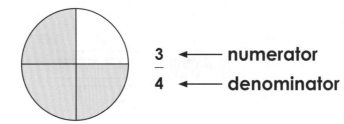

$\dfrac{3}{4}$ ← numerator
   ← denominator

In the fraction $\dfrac{3}{4}$, 3 is the **numerator** and 4 is the **denominator**.

The denominator tells us how many equal parts there are in a whole.

The numerator tells us how many of those equal parts are counted or used.

Let's Do

1. Name the numerator or denominator of each fraction.

   a) In $\dfrac{2}{5}$, the numerator is _____.

   b) In $\dfrac{4}{10}$, the denominator is _____.

   c) In $\dfrac{6}{7}$, the numerator is _____.

   d) In $\dfrac{6}{9}$, the denominator is _____.

P/B Chapter 11: Exercise 1, page 74

Comparing fractions

Let's Learn

These circles are of the same size.

a)

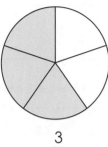 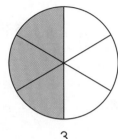 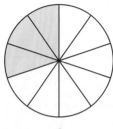

$$\frac{3}{5} \qquad \frac{3}{6} \qquad \frac{3}{10}$$

The fractions $\frac{3}{5}$, $\frac{3}{6}$ and $\frac{3}{10}$ have a **common numerator**.

□ is the smallest fraction.

□ is the greatest fraction.

When the numerators are common, the fraction with the greatest denominator is the □.

b)

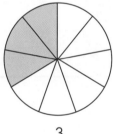 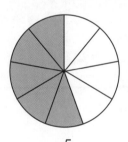 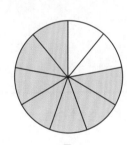

$$\frac{3}{9} \qquad \frac{5}{9} \qquad \frac{7}{9}$$

The fractions $\frac{3}{9}$, $\frac{5}{9}$ and $\frac{7}{9}$ have a **common denominator**.

□ is the smallest fraction.

□ is the greatest fraction.

When the denominators are common, the fraction with the greatest numerator is the □.

1. Arrange the fractions in order. Begin with the smallest.

   a) $\frac{1}{5}, \frac{1}{7}, \frac{1}{3}$ _____

   b) $\frac{2}{7}, \frac{2}{3}, \frac{2}{9}$ _____

   c) $\frac{5}{8}, \frac{7}{8}, \frac{4}{8}$ _____

   d) $\frac{5}{12}, \frac{9}{12}, \frac{4}{12}$ _____

P/B Chapter 11: Exercise 2, page 75

Practice 1

1. Complete the table.

	Fraction	Numerator	Denominator
a)	$\frac{1}{2}$		
b)	$\frac{3}{4}$		
c)	$\frac{5}{12}$		

2. Circle the greater fraction.

   a) $\frac{1}{4}, \frac{3}{4}$

   b) $\frac{2}{3}, \frac{2}{5}$

   c) $\frac{9}{12}, \frac{9}{10}$

Lesson 2 Equivalent Fractions

You will learn to...
- find equivalent fractions
- express a fraction in its simplest form
- compare using equivalent fractions

Understanding equivalent fractions

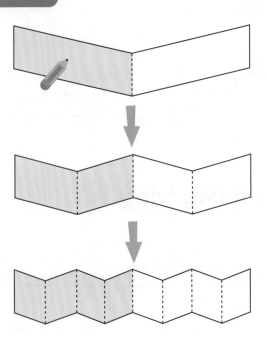

$\frac{1}{2}$ of the paper is shaded.

1 out of 2 equal parts

$\frac{2}{4}$ of the paper is shaded.

2 out of 4 equal parts

$\frac{4}{8}$ of the paper is shaded.

4 out of 8 equal parts

The fractions $\frac{1}{2}$, $\frac{2}{4}$ and $\frac{4}{8}$ have different numerators and denominators, but they are equal.

$\frac{1}{2}$		$\frac{1}{2}$	
$\frac{1}{4}$	$\frac{1}{4}$	$\frac{1}{4}$	$\frac{1}{4}$

$$\frac{1}{2} = \frac{2}{4} = \frac{4}{8}$$

$\frac{1}{8}$	$\frac{1}{8}$	$\frac{1}{8}$	$\frac{1}{8}$	$\frac{1}{8}$	$\frac{1}{8}$	$\frac{1}{8}$	$\frac{1}{8}$

 $\frac{1}{2}$, $\frac{2}{4}$ and $\frac{4}{8}$ are **equivalent fractions**.

$\frac{2}{4}$ and $\frac{4}{8}$ are different ways of writing $\frac{1}{2}$.

Two more equivalent fractions of $\frac{1}{2}$ are ▮.

1. Fill in the missing numerators.

$\frac{2}{3}$ of the bar is shaded.

a) $\frac{2}{3} = \frac{\boxed{}}{6}$

b) $\frac{2}{3} = \frac{\boxed{}}{9}$

c) $\frac{2}{3} = \frac{\boxed{}}{12}$

P/B Chapter 11: Exercise 3, pages 76–78

Finding equivalent fractions by multiplying

Let's Learn

What are the missing numerators and denominators?

a)

 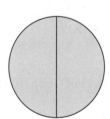  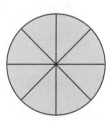

$$1 \quad = \quad \frac{2}{2} \quad = \quad \frac{3}{\boxed{}} \quad = \quad \frac{\boxed{}}{\boxed{}}$$

2 out of 2 equal parts is equal to 1 whole.

These are equivalent fractions.
They are different ways of writing 1 whole.

b)

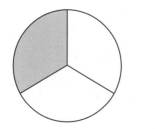 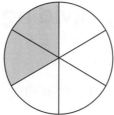 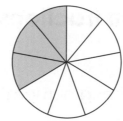 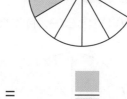

$$\frac{1}{3} = \frac{\square}{6} = \frac{3}{\square} = \frac{\square}{\square}$$

$$\overset{\times 2}{\frac{1}{3} = \frac{\square}{6}}\underset{\times 2}{}$$

$$\overset{\times 3}{\frac{1}{3} = \frac{3}{\square}}\underset{\times 3}{}$$

To find an equivalent fraction, we multiply the numerator and denominator by the same number.

c)

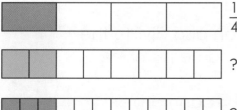

$\frac{1}{4}$

?

?

$$\overset{\times 2}{\frac{1}{4} = \frac{\square}{8}}\underset{\times 2}{}$$

$$\overset{\times 3}{\frac{1}{4} = \frac{3}{\square}}\underset{\times 3}{}$$

$$\frac{1}{4} = \frac{\square}{\square} = \frac{\square}{\square}$$

Let's Do

1. Write the missing numerators and denominators.

a) $\overset{\times 6}{\frac{1}{2} = \frac{\boxed{}}{12}}\underset{\times 6}{}$

b) $\overset{\times 3}{\frac{2}{3} = \frac{\boxed{}}{9}}\underset{\times 3}{}$

c) $\overset{\times 2}{\frac{1}{5} = \frac{\boxed{}}{10}}\underset{\times 2}{}$

d) $\frac{1}{6} = \frac{3}{\boxed{}}$

e) $\frac{3}{5} = \frac{6}{\boxed{}}$

f) $\frac{3}{4} = \frac{6}{\boxed{}}$

P/B Chapter 11: Exercise 4, pages 79–80

Finding equivalent fractions by dividing

Let's Learn

a) What are the missing numerators and denominators?

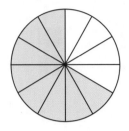 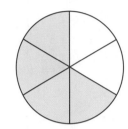 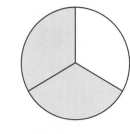

$$\frac{8}{12} \quad = \quad \frac{\blacksquare}{6} \quad = \quad \frac{2}{3}$$

$$\overset{\div 2}{\frac{8}{12}} = \frac{\blacksquare}{6} \qquad \overset{\div 4}{\frac{8}{12}} = \frac{2}{3}$$

$$\underset{\div 2}{} \qquad \underset{\div 4}{}$$

To find an equivalent fraction, we can also divide the numerator and denominator by the same number.

The numerator and denominator of $\frac{2}{3}$ cannot be further divided by the same number.

$\frac{2}{3}$ is the **simplest form** of $\frac{8}{12}$.

b) Is $\frac{3}{6}$ the simplest form of $\frac{6}{12}$?

No, we can further divide the numerator and denominator of $\frac{3}{6}$ by the same number.

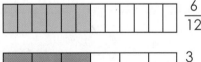 $\frac{6}{12}$

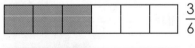 $\frac{3}{6}$

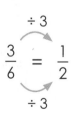 $\frac{1}{2}$

$$\overset{\div 3}{\frac{3}{6}} = \frac{1}{2}$$
$$\underset{\div 3}{}$$

Divide when you want to find the simplest form of a fraction.

$\frac{1}{2}$ is the simplest form of $\frac{6}{12}$.

Let's Do

1. Write the missing numerators and denominators.

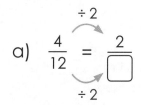

a) $\dfrac{4}{12} = \dfrac{2}{\boxed{}}$

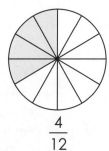 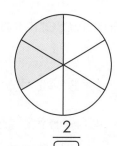

$\dfrac{4}{12} = \dfrac{2}{\boxed{}}$

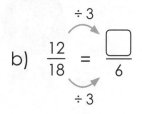

b) $\dfrac{12}{18} = \dfrac{\boxed{}}{6}$

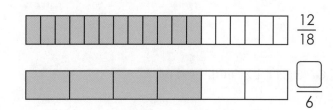

$\dfrac{12}{18}$ $\dfrac{\boxed{}}{6}$

2. Write the missing numerators and denominators.

a) $\overset{\div 2}{\underset{\div 2}{\dfrac{4}{8} = \dfrac{\boxed{}}{4}}}$

b) $\overset{\div 3}{\underset{\div 3}{\dfrac{9}{12} = \dfrac{\boxed{}}{4}}}$

c) $\overset{\div 2}{\underset{\div 2}{\dfrac{12}{16} = \dfrac{\boxed{}}{8}}}$

d) $\dfrac{16}{20} = \dfrac{4}{\boxed{}}$

e) $\dfrac{15}{25} = \dfrac{3}{\boxed{}}$

f) $\dfrac{10}{20} = \dfrac{1}{\boxed{}}$

3. Write the equivalent fractions of $\dfrac{6}{12}$.

$\dfrac{6}{12} = \dfrac{3}{\boxed{}} = \dfrac{2}{\boxed{}} = \dfrac{1}{\boxed{}}$

4. Write each fraction in its simplest form.

a) $\dfrac{2}{4} =$ _____

b) $\dfrac{6}{8} =$ _____

c) $\dfrac{5}{10} =$ _____

d) $\dfrac{3}{9} =$ _____

e) $\dfrac{10}{12} =$ _____

f) $\dfrac{4}{8} =$ _____

P/B Chapter 11: Exercises 5–6, pages 81–84

Are $\frac{2}{4}$ and $\frac{3}{6}$ equivalent fractions?

$\frac{2}{4} = \frac{1}{2}$, $\frac{3}{6} = \frac{1}{2}$

Yes, $\frac{1}{2}$ is the simplest form of $\frac{2}{4}$ and $\frac{3}{6}$.

No, I cannot find a number to multiply or divide the numerator and denominator of $\frac{2}{4}$ to get $\frac{3}{6}$.

Yen

Who is correct? Explain why.

Sam

Comparing using equivalent fractions

Let's Learn

a) These circles are of the same size.
   Which is greater, $\frac{3}{4}$ or $\frac{5}{8}$?

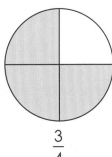

$\frac{3}{4}$ = $\frac{6}{8}$

It is easy to compare fractions when they have a common denominator.

$\frac{5}{8}$

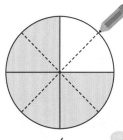

3 out of 4 equal parts is equivalent to ▢ out of 8 equal parts.

$$\overset{\times 2}{\underset{\times 2}{\frac{3}{4} = \frac{6}{8}}}$$

$\frac{6}{8}$ is greater than $\frac{5}{8}$.

So, $\frac{3}{4}$ is greater than $\frac{5}{8}$.

b) Which is smaller, $\frac{3}{5}$ or $\frac{1}{2}$?

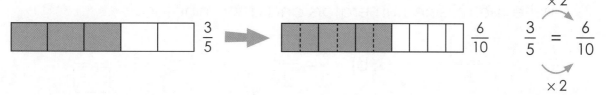

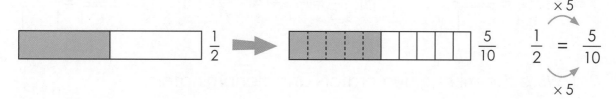

⬜ is smaller than ⬜.

So, ⬜ is smaller than ⬜.

Let's Do

1. Circle the greater fraction.

   a) $\frac{2}{3}$, $\frac{5}{6}$

   b) $\frac{3}{8}$, $\frac{1}{2}$

   c) $\frac{11}{12}$, $\frac{5}{6}$

   d) $\frac{1}{3}$, $\frac{5}{12}$

2. Circle the smaller fraction.

   a) $\frac{4}{5}$, $\frac{7}{10}$

   b) $\frac{3}{5}$, $\frac{4}{7}$

   $\frac{3}{5} = \frac{\square}{35}$ $\frac{4}{7} = \frac{\square}{35}$

   c) $\frac{2}{3}$, $\frac{3}{5}$

   d) $\frac{6}{7}$, $\frac{1}{3}$

Chapter 11: Exercise 7, page 85

Practice 2

1. Write the missing numerators and denominators.

   a) $\dfrac{1}{4} = \dfrac{\square}{8}$

   b) $\dfrac{3}{5} = \dfrac{\square}{15}$

   c) $\dfrac{3}{4} = \dfrac{9}{\square}$

   d) $\dfrac{2}{5} = \dfrac{4}{\square}$

   e) $\dfrac{1}{3} = \dfrac{\square}{6} = \dfrac{\square}{9}$

   f) $\dfrac{2}{3} = \dfrac{4}{\square} = \dfrac{6}{\square}$

2. Write the missing numerators and denominators.

   a) $\dfrac{6}{8} = \dfrac{3}{\square}$

   b) $\dfrac{6}{12} = \dfrac{3}{\square}$

   c) $\dfrac{4}{10} = \dfrac{\square}{5}$

   d) $\dfrac{6}{9} = \dfrac{\square}{3}$

   e) $\dfrac{3}{6} = \dfrac{\square}{2} = \dfrac{\square}{4}$

   f) $\dfrac{9}{12} = \dfrac{3}{\square} = \dfrac{6}{\square}$

3. Circle the smaller fraction.

   a) $\dfrac{5}{6}$, $\dfrac{9}{12}$

   b) $\dfrac{5}{7}$, $\dfrac{4}{5}$

   c) $\dfrac{3}{5}$, $\dfrac{5}{8}$

4. Circle the greatest fraction.

   a) $\dfrac{4}{7}$, $\dfrac{1}{7}$, $\dfrac{5}{7}$

   b) $\dfrac{2}{5}$, $\dfrac{2}{2}$, $\dfrac{2}{9}$

   c) $\dfrac{1}{2}$, $\dfrac{2}{6}$, $\dfrac{3}{4}$

Lesson 3 Adding Fractions

You will learn to...
- add fractions

Adding fractions with the same denominator

Let's Learn

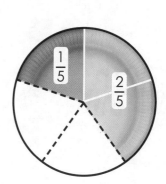

a) Pedro colors $\frac{1}{5}$ of a paper plate red.

Then, he colors $\frac{2}{5}$ of it blue.

What fraction of the paper plate does he color?

$\frac{1}{5}$ and $\frac{2}{5}$ are **like fractions**.
The denominators are the same.

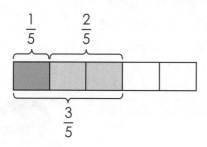

$\frac{1}{5} + \frac{2}{5} = \frac{3}{5}$

1 fifth and 2 fifths make 3 fifths.

He colors $\frac{3}{5}$ of the paper plate.

b) Add $\frac{3}{7}$ and $\frac{4}{7}$.

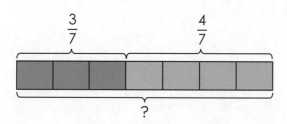

$\frac{3}{7} + \frac{4}{7} = \boxed{}$

$= \boxed{}$

3 sevenths and 4 sevenths make 1 whole.

95

c) Add $\frac{5}{8}$ and $\frac{1}{8}$.

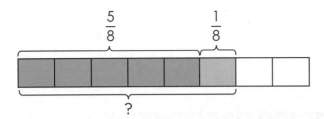

$\frac{5}{8} + \frac{1}{8} = \frac{\boxed{}}{8}$

$= \boxed{}$

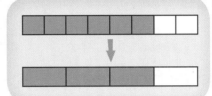

Think About It

$$\frac{5}{8} + \frac{1}{8} = ?$$

Add the numerators.
5 + 1 = 6
Add the denominators.
8 + 8 = 16
So, my answer is $\frac{6}{16} = \frac{3}{8}$.

Yen

No, you should not add the denominators because they show the total number of equal parts in a whole. We add 5 parts to 1 part to get 6 out of 8 equal parts.
$\frac{6}{8} = \frac{3}{4}$

Sam

Who is correct? Explain why.

Let's Do

1. Add. Write the answers in its simplest form.

a) $\frac{1}{9} + \frac{4}{9} = $ _____

b) $\frac{2}{7} + \frac{2}{7} = $ _____

c) $\frac{1}{8} + \frac{1}{8} = \frac{\boxed{}}{8}$

$= $ _____

d) $\frac{5}{12} + \frac{7}{12} = \frac{\boxed{}}{12}$

$= $ _____

PB Chapter 11: Exercise 8, pages 86–87

Adding fractions with different denominators

Let's Learn

a) Cassie ate $\frac{1}{4}$ of a grapefruit.

Diego ate $\frac{3}{8}$ of the same grapefruit.

What fraction of the grapefruit did they eat altogether?

$\frac{1}{4}$ and $\frac{3}{8}$ do not have the same denominator.

Find an equivalent fraction of $\frac{1}{4}$ that has the same denominator as $\frac{3}{8}$.

$$\frac{1}{4} = \frac{2}{8} \qquad \frac{3}{8}$$

$$\frac{1}{4} + \frac{3}{8} = \frac{2}{8} + \frac{3}{8}$$
$$= \frac{5}{8}$$

They ate ☐ of the grapefruit altogether.

b) Add $\frac{1}{6}$ and $\frac{1}{3}$.

Find an equivalent fraction of $\frac{1}{3}$ that has the same denominator as $\frac{1}{6}$.

$$\frac{1}{6} \qquad \frac{1}{3} = \boxed{}$$

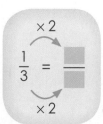

$$\frac{1}{6} + \frac{1}{3} = \frac{1}{6} + \frac{\boxed{}}{6}$$
$$= \frac{\boxed{}}{6}$$
$$= \boxed{}$$

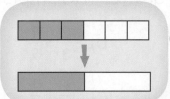

Remember to write your answer in its simplest form.

1. Add. Write the answer in its simplest form.

a) $\dfrac{5}{6} + \dfrac{1}{12} = \dfrac{\boxed{}}{12} + \dfrac{1}{12}$

$= \underline{}$

b) $\dfrac{1}{6} + \dfrac{2}{3} = \dfrac{1}{6} + \dfrac{\boxed{}}{6}$

$= \underline{}$

c) $\dfrac{1}{10} + \dfrac{2}{5} = \dfrac{1}{10} + \dfrac{\boxed{}}{10}$

$= \dfrac{\boxed{}}{10}$

$= \underline{}$

d) $\dfrac{1}{4} + \dfrac{5}{12} = \dfrac{\boxed{}}{12} + \dfrac{5}{12}$

$= \dfrac{\boxed{}}{12}$

$= \underline{}$

P/B Chapter 11: Exercise 9, pages 88–89

Practice 3

1. Add. Write the answer in its simplest form.

a) $\dfrac{1}{3} + \dfrac{1}{3}$

b) $\dfrac{1}{9} + \dfrac{7}{9}$

c) $\dfrac{2}{7} + \dfrac{3}{7}$

d) $\dfrac{1}{4} + \dfrac{3}{4}$

e) $\dfrac{1}{2} + \dfrac{1}{2}$

f) $\dfrac{6}{11} + \dfrac{4}{11}$

g) $\dfrac{1}{8} + \dfrac{3}{8}$

h) $\dfrac{1}{12} + \dfrac{5}{12}$

i) $\dfrac{1}{6} + \dfrac{3}{6}$

2. Add. Write the answer in its simplest form.

a) $\dfrac{1}{2} + \dfrac{1}{4}$

b) $\dfrac{2}{3} + \dfrac{1}{9}$

c) $\dfrac{1}{8} + \dfrac{3}{4}$

d) $\dfrac{3}{10} + \dfrac{2}{5}$

e) $\dfrac{4}{9} + \dfrac{1}{3}$

f) $\dfrac{1}{5} + \dfrac{3}{10}$

g) $\dfrac{3}{4} + \dfrac{1}{12}$

h) $\dfrac{1}{2} + \dfrac{4}{8}$

i) $\dfrac{1}{3} + \dfrac{3}{6}$

Lesson 4   Subtracting Fractions

You will learn to...
- subtract fractions

Subtracting fractions with the same denominator

Let's Learn

a)   David had $\frac{7}{9}$ of a pizza.

He ate $\frac{2}{9}$ of the pizza.

What fraction of the pizza was left?

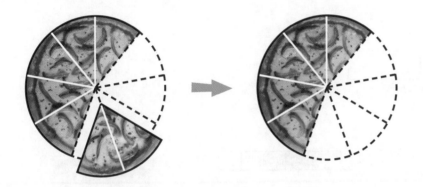

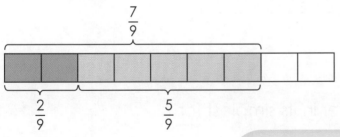

 $\frac{7}{9} - \frac{2}{9} = \frac{5}{9}$

$\frac{5}{9}$ of the pizza was left.

Subtracting 2 ninths from 7 ninths gives 5 ninths.

b) Subtract $\frac{3}{10}$ from 1.

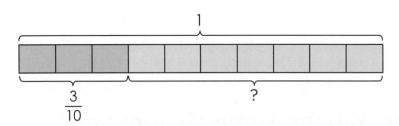

$\frac{3}{10}$?

$1 - \frac{3}{10} = \boxed{} - \frac{3}{10}$

$\phantom{1 - \frac{3}{10}} = \boxed{}$

1 whole = ten of 10 equal parts

$1 = \frac{10}{10}$

c) Subtract $\frac{1}{6}$ from $\frac{5}{6}$.

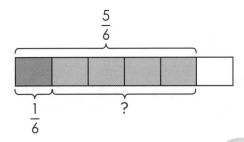

$\frac{5}{6}$

$\frac{1}{6}$?

$\frac{5}{6} - \frac{1}{6} = \dfrac{\boxed{}}{6}$

$\phantom{\frac{5}{6} - \frac{1}{6}} = \boxed{}$

Let's Do

1. Subtract. Write the answer in its simplest form.

a) $\frac{4}{5} - \frac{1}{5} =$ _____

b) $1 - \frac{2}{9} = \dfrac{\boxed{}}{9} - \frac{2}{9}$

$= $ _____

c) $\frac{5}{8} - \frac{1}{8} = \dfrac{\boxed{}}{8}$

$= $ _____

d) $\frac{8}{12} - \frac{5}{12} = \dfrac{\boxed{}}{12}$

$= $ _____

Chapter 11: Exercise 10, pages 90–91

Subtracting fractions with different denominators

Let's Learn

a) Suzy had $\frac{7}{10}$ of a pizza. She gave away $\frac{3}{5}$ of the pizza. What fraction of the pizza was left?

Find an equivalent fraction of $\frac{3}{5}$ that has the same denominator as $\frac{7}{10}$.

 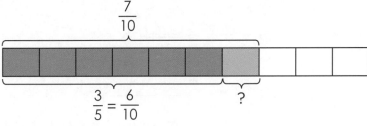

$$\frac{7}{10} - \frac{3}{5} = \frac{7}{10} - \frac{6}{10}$$

$$= \frac{1}{10}$$

 ▢ of the pizza was left.

b) Subtract $\frac{5}{12}$ from $\frac{3}{4}$.

Find an equivalent fraction of $\frac{3}{4}$ that has the same denominator as $\frac{5}{12}$.

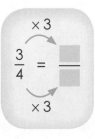

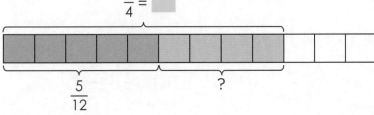

$$\frac{3}{4} - \frac{5}{12} = \frac{▢}{12} - \frac{5}{12}$$

$$= \frac{▢}{12}$$

$$= ▢$$

Remember to write your answer in its simplest form.

1. Subtract. Write the answer in its simplest form.

a) $\dfrac{3}{4} - \dfrac{1}{8} = \dfrac{\boxed{}}{8} - \dfrac{1}{8}$

$= \underline{}$

b) $\dfrac{5}{6} - \dfrac{1}{2} = \dfrac{5}{6} - \dfrac{\boxed{}}{6}$

$= \underline{}$

c) $\dfrac{7}{10} - \dfrac{1}{2} = \dfrac{7}{10} - \dfrac{\boxed{}}{10}$

$= \dfrac{\boxed{}}{10}$

$= \underline{}$

d) $\dfrac{5}{6} - \dfrac{7}{12} = \dfrac{\boxed{}}{12} - \dfrac{7}{12}$

$= \dfrac{\boxed{}}{12}$

$= \underline{}$

P/B Chapter 11: Exercise 11, pages 92–93

Practice 4

1. Subtract. Write the answer in its simplest form.

a) $\dfrac{4}{5} - \dfrac{1}{5}$

b) $\dfrac{2}{3} - \dfrac{1}{3}$

c) $\dfrac{10}{11} - \dfrac{7}{11}$

d) $1 - \dfrac{2}{9}$

e) $\dfrac{7}{10} - \dfrac{4}{10}$

f) $\dfrac{8}{12} - \dfrac{3}{12}$

g) $\dfrac{3}{4} - \dfrac{1}{4}$

h) $\dfrac{5}{6} - \dfrac{1}{6}$

i) $\dfrac{7}{8} - \dfrac{5}{8}$

2. Subtract. Write the answer in its simplest form.

a) $\dfrac{5}{9} - \dfrac{1}{3}$

b) $\dfrac{11}{12} - \dfrac{1}{2}$

c) $\dfrac{4}{5} - \dfrac{7}{10}$

d) $\dfrac{7}{10} - \dfrac{2}{5}$

e) $\dfrac{5}{6} - \dfrac{1}{2}$

f) $\dfrac{1}{3} - \dfrac{1}{12}$

g) $\dfrac{1}{2} - \dfrac{1}{10}$

h) $\dfrac{3}{4} - \dfrac{7}{12}$

i) $\dfrac{4}{8} - \dfrac{1}{2}$

Lesson 5　Problem Solving

Word problems

Let's Learn

Jude ate $\frac{1}{3}$ of a custard tart.

What fraction of the tart was left?

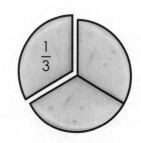

1 **Understand** the problem.

> What was eaten?
> What fraction of the tart was eaten?
> What do I have to find?
> What information is not useful?

2 **Plan** what to do.

> I can **use the picture given**.

3 Work out the **Answer**.

$$1 - \frac{1}{3} = \frac{3}{3} - \frac{1}{3}$$
$$= \frac{2}{3}$$

4 **Check**
Did you answer the question?
Is your answer correct?

> He ate 1 of 3 equal pieces of the tart.
> $3 - 1 = 2$
> 2 of 3 equal pieces of the tart were left.
> $\frac{2}{3}$ of the tart was left.
> $\frac{1}{3}$ and $\frac{2}{3}$ make 1 whole.
> My answer is correct.

☑ 1. Understand
☑ 2. Plan
☑ 3. Answer
☑ 4. Check

1. Vera ate $\frac{1}{4}$ of an orange. Her sister ate $\frac{3}{8}$ of the same orange.

   What fraction of the orange did they eat altogether?

Add _____ and _____ to find the fraction of the orange they ate altogether.

☐ 1. Understand
☐ 2. Plan
☐ 3. Answer
☐ 4. Check

They ate _____ of the orange altogether.

Let's Learn

Sonia ate $\frac{3}{8}$ of a melon.

William ate $\frac{1}{2}$ of the same melon.

Who ate a bigger portion of the melon?

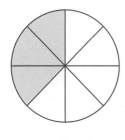

$\frac{3}{8}$

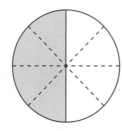

$\frac{1}{2} = \frac{\boxed{}}{8}$

$\frac{1}{2} = \frac{\boxed{}}{8}$ × 4

⬛ is greater than ⬛.

⬛ ate a bigger portion of the melon.

☑ 1. Understand
☑ 2. Plan
☑ 3. Answer
☑ 4. Check

1. Saul colored $\frac{2}{10}$ of this shape green.

   He colored $\frac{3}{5}$ of it blue.

   Did Saul color a smaller portion of the shape green or blue?

   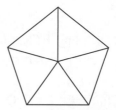

   $\frac{2}{10}$ = _____

   _____ is smaller than _____.

   | ☐ 1. Understand |
   | ☐ 2. Plan |
   | ☐ 3. Answer |
   | ☐ 4. Check |

   Saul colored a smaller portion of the shape _____.

P/B Chapter 11: Exercise 12, pages 94–96

Practice 5

Solve the word problems. Draw bar models to help you.
Show your work clearly.

1. Betty has a can of paint.

   She uses $\frac{1}{2}$ of it to paint a table and $\frac{1}{8}$ of it to paint a chair.

   What fraction of the paint does she use altogether?

2. Zelia has $\frac{3}{4}$ of an apple. She eats $\frac{1}{2}$ of the apple.
   How much of the apple is left?

3. Matt spent $\frac{4}{9}$ of his pocket money and saved the rest.

   What fraction of his pocket money did he save?

4. A watermelon was cut into 8 equal slices.

   Ahmed ate 2 slices. Latif ate $\frac{1}{4}$ of the watermelon.
   Who ate more?

Create Your Own!

Write the missing fractions. Then, solve the word problem.
Show your work clearly.

Mr. Lee painted ____ of a wall red.

His daughter painted ____ of the same wall white.

Was a greater fraction of the wall painted red or white?

Mind stretcher

Let's Learn

$$\frac{2}{\boxed{}} + \frac{2}{\boxed{}} = 1$$

What are the two possible pairs of denominators that
are missing above?

1 **Understand** the problem.

> What is the sum of
> the fractions?
> What is missing?
> How many possible pairs of
> denominators are there?

2 **Plan** what to do.

> I can **guess and check** to find
> the denominators.

3 Work out the Answer.

Guess 1

	Same denominator		$\frac{2}{\boxed{}} + \frac{2}{\boxed{}} = ?$	Sum equal to 1?
a)	2	2	$\frac{2}{2} + \frac{2}{2} = 1 + 1$ $= 2$	✗
b)	4	4	$\frac{2}{4} + \frac{2}{4} = \frac{1}{2} + \frac{1}{2}$ $= 1$	✓

106

Check

Check

Did you answer the question? Is your answer correct?

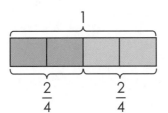

$\frac{2}{4}$ and $\frac{2}{4}$ make 1 whole. My answer is correct.

The denominators can be 4 and 4.

3 Work out the Answer.

Guess 2

	Different denominator		$\dfrac{2}{\square} + \dfrac{2}{\square} = ?$	Sum equal to 1?
a)	2	4	$\frac{2}{2} + \frac{2}{4} = 1 + \frac{1}{2}$ $= 1\frac{1}{2}$	✗
b)	6	3	$\frac{2}{6} + \frac{2}{3} = \frac{1}{3} + \frac{2}{3}$ $= 1$	✓

Check

Did you answer the question? Is your answer correct?

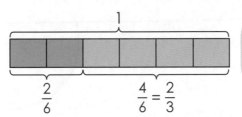

$\frac{2}{6}$ and $\frac{2}{3}$ also make 1 whole. My answer is correct.

The denominators can also be 3 and 6.

☑ 1. Understand
☑ 2. Plan
☑ 3. Answer
☑ 4. Check

 Review 5, pages 97–104

Time

1. a)

    _____**5**_____ minutes after
    2 o'clock.
    The time is ___**2:05**___.

    b)

    _____**15**_____ minutes after
    4 o'clock.
    The time is ___**4:15**___.

    c)

    ▨ minutes before
    4 o'clock.
    The time is ▨.

    d)

    ▨ minutes before
    8 o'clock.
    The time is ▨.

2. a) Mr. Lin's family eats breakfast at 8:30 a.m.

    b) Mia ends her school day at 1:30 p.m.

c) 1 hour after noon is
1:00 ▢ .

d) 4 hours after midnight is
4:00 ▢ .

e) 6 hours before noon is
6:00 ▢ .

We use a.m. for the time from just after midnight to just before noon.

We use p.m. for the time from just after noon to just before midnight.

3. a)

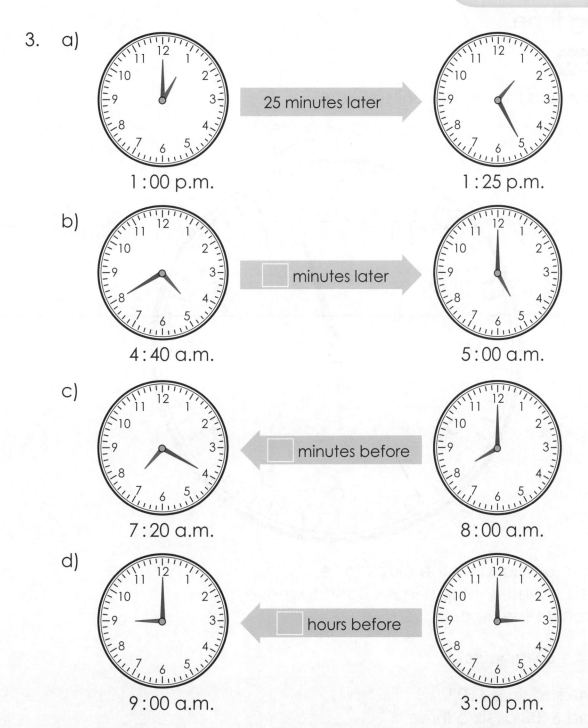

1:00 p.m.   25 minutes later   1:25 p.m.

b)

4:40 a.m.   ▢ minutes later   5:00 a.m.

c)

7:20 a.m.   ▢ minutes before   8:00 a.m.

d)

9:00 a.m.   ▢ hours before   3:00 p.m.

Lesson 1   Hours and Minutes

You will learn to...
- tell and write time
- express hours and minutes in minutes
- express minutes in hours and minutes
- add and subtract in hours and minutes

Reading time

Let's Learn

The hour and minute are units of time.

There are 60 marks on the clock face.
It takes 1 minute for the minute hand to move from
one mark to the next.

| 1 hour = 60 minutes |

The time shown is 6:03.
We read 6:03 as six o three.

It is 5 minutes after 7 o'clock in
the morning.
It is 5 minutes **past** 7.
It is 7 : 05 a.m.
Sam is brushing his teeth.

It is 8 minutes after 12 o'clock in
the afternoon.
It is 8 minutes past noon.
It is 12 : 08 p.m.
Sam is in his classroom.

It is 10 minutes before 8 o'clock
at night.
It is 10 minutes **to** 8.
It is 7 : 50 p.m.
Sam is having dinner with his family.

It is 6 minutes before 12 o'clock
at night.
It is 6 minutes to midnight.
It is 11 : 54 p.m.
Sam is sleeping.

$60 - 6 = 54$

1. Fill in the blanks.

a)

2:00 p.m.

_____ minutes past 2

The time is _____.

b)

_____ minutes to 9

The time is _____.

9:00 a.m.

2. Draw the minute hand to show the time.

a)

4:38

b)

9:52

c)

23 minutes past 6

d)

17 minutes to 12

112

3. a) Find out how many times you can write your name in 1 minute.

   b) Estimate how many times you can write your name in 1 hour.

P/B Chapter 12: Exercise 1, pages 105–106

Duration of time

Let's Learn

a)

How long would I take to run 3 kilometers?

8 : 20
20 minutes past 8

20 minutes

17 minutes

8 : 37
23 minutes to 9

David started running at 8 : 20 a.m.
He ran 3 kilometers.
He finished at 8 : 37 a.m.
He took 17 minutes to run 3 kilometers.

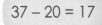

5 ... 10 ... 15 ... 17

37 − 20 = 17

b) What time is 36 minutes after 11:30 a.m.?

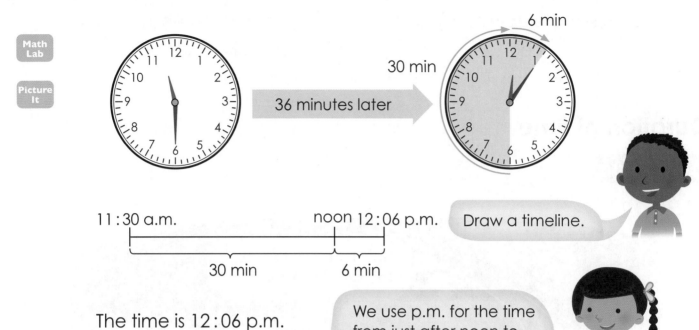

11:30 a.m.   noon 12:06 p.m.

        30 min   6 min

The time is 12:06 p.m.

Draw a timeline.

We use p.m. for the time from just after noon to just before midnight.

c) How long is it from 10:25 a.m. to 11:40 a.m.?

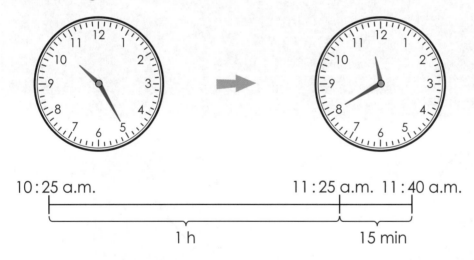

10:25 a.m.   11:25 a.m. 11:40 a.m.

              1 h   15 min

1 hour after 10:25 a.m. is 11:25 a.m.
15 minutes after 11:25 a.m. is 11:40 a.m.
It is 1 hour 15 minutes from 10:25 a.m. to 11:40 a.m.

$40 - 25 = 15$

114

d) How long is it from 10:45 a.m. to 12:10 p.m.?

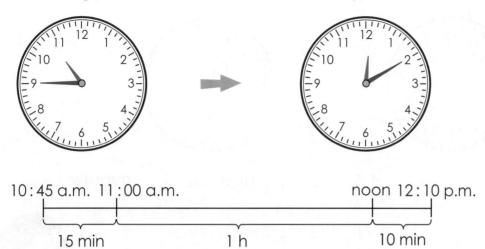

10:45 a.m. 11:00 a.m.   noon 12:10 p.m.

15 min   1 h   10 min

15 minutes after 10:45 a.m. is 11:00 a.m.
1 hour after 11:00 a.m. is noon.
10 minutes after noon is 12:10 p.m.
It is 1 hour 25 minutes from 10:45 a.m. to 12:10 p.m.

15 min + 10 min = 25 min

Let's Do

1. Fill in the blanks.

   a) How many minutes are there from 1:15 p.m. to 1:42 p.m.?

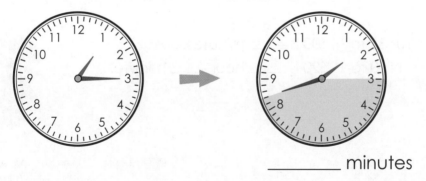

   _____ minutes

   b) How many hours are there from 3:18 p.m. to 8:18 p.m.?

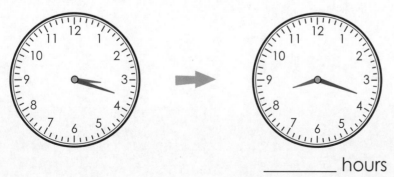

   _____ hours

c) How long is it from 11:15 a.m. to 12:30 p.m.?

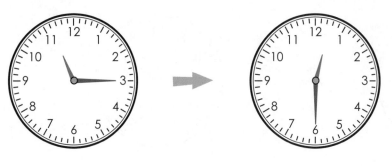

_____ hour _____ minutes

11:15 to 12:15 is _____ hour.
12:15 to 12:30 is _____ minutes.

d) How long is it from 10:35 a.m. to 12:20 p.m.?

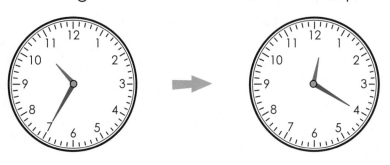

_____ hour _____ minutes

10:35 to 11:00 is _____ minutes.
11:00 to 12:20 is _____ hour _____ minutes.

PB Chapter 12: Exercise 2, pages 107–108

Expressing hours and minutes in minutes

Let's Learn

a) Mary took 1 hour 35 minutes to complete a jigsaw puzzle.
What is the time in minutes?

1 hour 35 minutes is ☐ minutes more than 1 hour.

```
                1 h = 60 min
1 h 35 min
                35 min
```

1 hr 35 min = 60 min + 35 min
= 95 min

Mary took 95 minutes to complete the jigsaw puzzle.

b) What is 2 hours 18 minutes in minutes?

```
              ☐ h = ☐ min
2 h 18 min
              ☐ min
```

1 h = 60 min
2 h = ☐ min

2 h 18 min = ☐ min + ☐ min
= ☐ min

Let's Do

1. Express in minutes.

a) 2 h = _____ min

b) 2 h 10 min = _____ min

c) 2 h 45 min = _____ min

d) 3 h = _____ min

e) 3 h 5 min = _____ min

f) 3 h 15 min = _____ min

Expressing minutes in hours and minutes

Let's Learn

a) Mrs. Lin sewed 4 sets of curtains.
She took 50 minutes to sew each set of curtains.
Find the total time she took in hours and minutes.

50 min × 4 = 200 min

200 min
- 180 min = 3 h
- 20 min

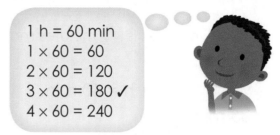

1 h = 60 min
1 × 60 = 60
2 × 60 = 120
3 × 60 = 180 ✓
4 × 60 = 240

200 min = 3 h + 20 min
= 3 h 20 min

She took 3 hours and 20 minutes.

b) What is 330 minutes in hours and minutes?

330 min
- 300 min = 5 h
- ▢ min

60, 120, 180, 240,
300, 360 ✓

330 min = ▢ h + ▢ min
= ▢ h ▢ min

Let's Do

1. Express in hours and minutes.

a) 70 min = ____ h ____ min

b) 85 min = ____ h ____ min

c) 100 min = ____ h ____ min

d) 125 min = ____ h ____ min

e) 160 min = ____ h ____ min

f) 210 min = ____ h ____ min

2. The table shows the time taken by three children to paint a picture.

a) Who took the longest time?

_____

b) Who took the shortest time?

_____

Name	Time taken
Anne	1 h 15 min
Jane	2 h 5 min
Sheila	80 min

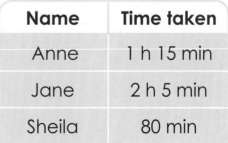

P/B Chapter 12: Exercise 3, pages 109–110

Adding and subtracting hours and minutes

Rachel spent 1 hour 20 minutes on her Spanish homework.
She spent 2 hours 35 minutes on her English homework.

a) How much time did she spend on homework altogether?

1 h 20 min + 2 h 35 min = ▢ h ▢ min

First, add the hours.
Then, add the minutes.

1 h 20 min $\xrightarrow{+\,2\,h}$ 3 h 20 min $\xrightarrow{+\,35\,min}$ 3 h 55 min

Rachel spent 3 hours 55 minutes on homework altogether.

b) How much more time did Rachel spend on her English homework?

2 h 35 min – 1 h 20 min = ▢ h ▢ min

First, subtract the hours.
Then, subtract the minutes.

2 h 35 min $\xrightarrow{-\,1\,h}$ 1 h 35 min $\xrightarrow{-\,20\,min}$ 1 h 15 min

Rachel spent 1 hour 15 minutes more on her English homework.

Let's Do

1. Add or subtract.

   a) 2 h 40 min + 5 min = _____ h _____ min

   b) 3 h 15 min – 2 h = _____ h _____ min

   c) 1 h 25 min + 2 h 15 min = _____ h _____ min

   d) 3 h 50 min – 1 h 35 min = _____ h _____ min

119

a) 3 h 20 min + 2 h 45 min = ☐ h ☐ min

Method 1

3 h 20 min $\xrightarrow{\ +\ 2\ h\ }$ 5 h 20 min $\xrightarrow{\ +\ 45\ min\ }$ 5 h 65 min = 6 h 5 min

65 min = 60 min + 5 min

Method 2

3 h 20 min $\Big\langle$ 3 h = 180 min
20 min

2 h 45 min $\Big\langle$ 2 h = 120 min
45 min

3 h 20 min + 2 h 45 min = 200 min + 165 min
                       = 365 min
                       = 6 h 5 min

6 × 60 = 360
360 min = 6 h

b) 3 h 20 min – 2 h 45 min = ☐ h ☐ min

Method 1

3 h 20 min $\xrightarrow{\ -\ 2\ h\ }$ 1 h 20 min $\xrightarrow{\ -\ 45\ min\ }$?

$\underbrace{\text{1 h 20 min}}_{\text{80 min}}$ $\xrightarrow{\ -\ 45\ min\ }$ 35 min

Method 2

3 h 20 min – 2 h 45 min = 200 min – 165 min
                       = 35 min

1. Add or subtract.

   a) 2 h 40 min + 2 h 25 min = _____ h _____ min

   b) 4 h 15 min – 1 h 50 min = _____ h _____ min

P/B Chapter 12: Exercise 4, pages 111–112

Word problems

Let's Learn

a) A supermarket is open from 10:15 a.m. to 9:30 p.m. every day.
   For how long is the supermarket open in a day?

Method 1

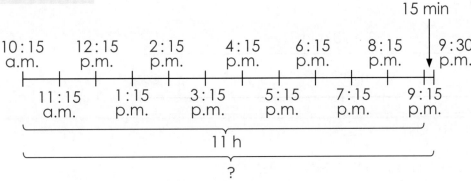

11 h + 15 min = 11 h 15 min

Method 2

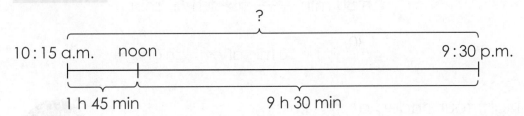

1 h 45 min + 9 h 30 min = ▢ h ▢ min

1 h 45 min $\xrightarrow{+9\,h}$ 10 h 45 min $\xrightarrow{+30\,min}$ 10 h 75 min = 11 h 15 min

The supermarket is open for ▢ hours ▢ minutes in a day.

b) A night tour began at 10:30 p.m. and lasted 3 hours 20 minutes.
    When did the night tour end?

Method 1

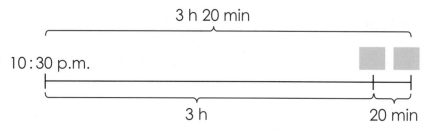

3 h 20 min

10:30 p.m.

3 h   20 min

3 hours after 10:30 p.m. is 1:30 a.m.
20 minutes after 1:30 a.m. is 1:50 a.m.

We use a.m. for the time
from just after midnight
to just before noon.

Method 2

3 h 20 min

10:30 p.m.   midnight

1 h 30 min   ?

3 h 20 min – 1 h 30 min = ⬚ h ⬚ min

$$3 \text{ h } 20 \text{ min} \xrightarrow{-1\text{ h}} 2 \text{ h } 20 \text{ min} \xrightarrow{-30\text{ min}} ?$$

$$1 \text{ h } 80 \text{ min} \xrightarrow{-30\text{ min}} 1 \text{ h } 50 \text{ min}$$

What is 1 h 50 min after midnight?

The night tour ended at ⬚ a.m.

c) Karen took a flight from Singapore to Osaka. The flight took 6 hours 15 minutes. If she arrived in Osaka at 2:35 p.m., what time did the plane leave Singapore?

Method 1

Draw a timeline and mark the end time first.

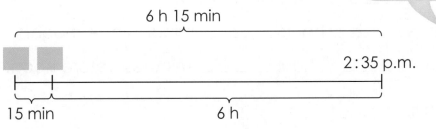

6 hours before 2:35 p.m. is ▢.
15 minutes before ▢ is ▢.

Work backwards from the end time.

Method 2

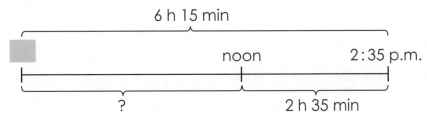

6 h 15 min − 2 h 35 min = ▢ h ▢ min

6 h 15 min $\xrightarrow{-2\,h}$ 4 h 15 min $\xrightarrow{-35\,min}$?

3 h 75 min $\xrightarrow{-35\,min}$ 3 h 40 min

What is 3 h 40 min before noon?

The plane left Singapore at ▢.

Let's Do

1. Fill in the blanks.

10:45 a.m.   noon   2:00 p.m.   3:30 p.m.

a) 2:00 p.m. is _____ hours after noon.

b) 3:30 p.m. is _____ hours _____ minutes after noon.

c) 10:45 a.m. is _____ hour _____ minutes before noon.

2. Fill in the blanks.

9:10 p.m.   midnight   4:00 a.m.   6:40 a.m.

a) 4:00 a.m. is _____ hours after midnight.

b) 6:40 a.m. is _____ hours _____ minutes after midnight.

c) 9:10 p.m. is _____ hours _____ minutes before midnight.

Solve the word problems. Draw a timeline to help you.
Show your work clearly.

3. A plane left Singapore at 8:00 a.m. It arrived in Penang at
9:05 a.m. on the same day. How long did the journey take?

4. Jasmine went to the market at 7:15 a.m. She came home
1 hour 45 minutes later. When did she come home?

5. Sally took 1 hour 10 minutes to do her homework. She finished
doing her homework at 9:40 p.m. When did she start?

P/B Chapter 12: Exercise 5, pages 113–114

Let's Do

Practice 1

1. What time is shown on each clock?

   a)

   b)

2. This clock is 5 minutes slow. What is the correct time?

3. Express in minutes.

   a) 2 h 12 min

   b) 4 h 7 min

4. Express in hours and minutes.

   a) 108 min

   b) 259 min

5. Add or subtract.

   a) 1 h 45 min + 2 h   b) 3 h 40 min – 2 h
   c) 2 h 15 min + 45 min   d) 3 h – 1 h 45 min
   e) 1 h 30 min + 1 h 50 min   f) 2 h 10 min – 1 h 30 min

6. Find the duration.

   a) From 4:40 a.m. to 11:55 a.m.
   b) From 5:45 p.m. to 7:00 p.m.
   c) From 10:05 p.m. to 12:00 midnight.
   d) From 2:40 p.m. to 3:25 p.m.

7. Mrs. Li went shopping at 10:20 a.m.
   She returned home 4 hours later.
   What time did she return home?

8. Jacob took 5 hours 45 minutes to drive from
   Singapore to Kuala Lumpur.
   He arrived there at 2:15 p.m.
   What time did he leave Singapore?

Lesson 2   Other Units of Time

You will learn to...
- express years and months in months
- express months in years and months
- express weeks and days in days
- express days in weeks and days

Expressing years and months in months

Let's Learn

The year, month, week and day are units of time.

a)   Roger is 2 years and 8 months old.
How old is he in months?

2 years 8 months
- 2 years = 24 months
- 8 months

1 year = 12 months
2 years = 24 months

  2 years 8 months = 24 months + 8 months
= 32 months

Roger is 32 months old.

b)   What is 3 years and 6 months in months?

3 years 6 months
- 3 years = 36 months
- 6 months

3 years 6 months = 36 months + 6 months
= 42 months

Expressing months in years and months

Let's Learn

a) Kim is 40 months old.
How old is she in years and months?

40 months
— 36 months = 3 years
— 4 months

+ 12 + 12 + 12
12, 24, 36, 48

40 months = 3 years + 4 months
          = 3 years 4 months

Kim is 3 years and 4 months old.

b) What is 56 months in years and months?

56 months
— ☐ months = ☐ years
— ☐ months

+ 12 + 12 + 12 + 12
12, 24, 36, 48, 60

56 months = ☐ years + ☐ months
          = ☐ years ☐ months

Let's Do

1. Fill in the blanks.

   a) 2 years = _____ months

   b) 5 years 4 months = _____ months

   c) 48 months = _____ years

   d) 39 months = _____ years _____ months

PB Chapter 12: Exercise 6, pages 115–116

Expressing weeks and days in days

Let's Learn

a) Karl stayed in Japan for 2 weeks and 3 days.
How many days did he stay in Japan?

2 weeks 3 days
- 2 weeks = 14 days
- 3 days

1 week = 7 days
2 weeks = 14 days

2 weeks 3 days = 14 days + 3 days
= 17 days

Karl stayed in Japan for 17 days.

b) What is 3 weeks and 2 days in days?

3 weeks 2 days
- ▢ weeks = ▢ days
- ▢ days

7 × 3 = 21

3 weeks 2 days = ▢ days + ▢ days
= ▢ days

Expressing days in weeks and days

Let's Learn

a) Kelly stayed in India for 18 days.
How many weeks and days did she stay in India?

18 days
- 14 days = 2 weeks
- 4 days

✓
7, 14, 21

18 days = 2 weeks + 4 days
= 2 weeks 4 days

Kelly stayed in India for 2 weeks and 4 days.

b) What is 26 days in weeks and days?

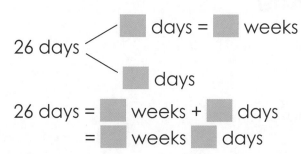

7, 14, 21, 28 ✓

26 days = ☐ weeks + ☐ days

= ☐ weeks ☐ days

Let's Do

1. Fill in the blanks.

   a) 3 weeks = _____ days

   b) 4 weeks 4 days = _____ days

   c) 30 days = _____ weeks _____ days

   d) 52 days = _____ weeks _____ days

P/B Chapter 12: Exercise 7, pages 117–118

Practice 2

1. Fill in the blanks.

   a) 1 year 9 months = ____ months

   b) 3 years 11 months = ____ months

   c) 30 months = ____ years ____ months

   d) 63 months = ____ years ____ months

   e) 4 weeks = ____ days

   f) 2 weeks 5 days = ____ days

   g) 40 days = ____ weeks ____ days

   h) 29 days = ____ weeks ____ day

Lesson 3   Problem Solving
Word problems

Let's Learn

Daniel slept for 8 hours and 25 minutes.
He woke up at 6:15 a.m.
Rachel had gone to bed 1 hour 40 minutes after Daniel.

a)   What time did Daniel go to bed?
b)   What time did Rachel go to bed?

1 **Understand** the problem.

How long did Daniel sleep?
What time did he wake up?
What do I have to find?

2 **Plan** what to do.

I can **draw** a timeline and **work backwards**.

3 Work out the **Answer**.

a)   **Method 1**

```
?   10:15 p.m.                          6:15 a.m.
├───┼──────────────────────────────────┤
 25 min                8 h
```

8 hours before 6:15 a.m. is 10:15 p.m.
25 minutes before 10:15 p.m. is 9:50 p.m.

Method 2

6:15 a.m. is 6 h 15 min after midnight.

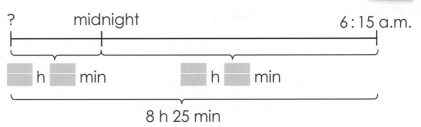

```
?          midnight                    6:15 a.m.
├──────────────┼───────────────────────┤
```

8 h 25 min − 6 h 15 min = 2 h 10 min
2 h 10 min before midnight is 9:50 p.m.
Daniel went to bed at 9:50 p.m.

130

b)

Method 1

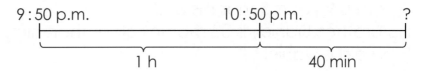

1 hour after 9:50 p.m. is 10:50 p.m.

40 minutes after 10:50 p.m. is [ ] p.m.

Method 2

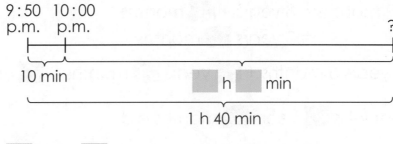

[ ] hour [ ] minutes after 10:00 p.m.

is [ ] p.m.

Rachel went to bed at [ ] p.m.

4 **Check**
Did you answer
the question?
Is your answer
reasonable?

Rachel went to bed later than Daniel.
[ ] p.m. is later than 9:50 p.m.
My answer is reasonable.

☑ 1. Understand
☑ 2. Plan
☑ 3. Answer
☑ 4. Check

Let's Do

1. David took part in a race. He started running at 7:45 a.m.
   After running for 2 hours 20 minutes, he took a break before
   starting to run again at 10:15 a.m. How long was his break?

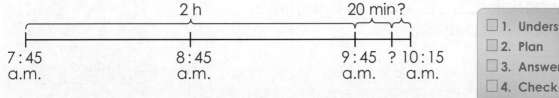

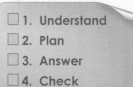

☐ 1. Understand
☐ 2. Plan
☐ 3. Answer
☐ 4. Check

131

Let's Learn

Adam is 9 years 5 months old.
His brother, Daniel, is 39 months older than him.
How old is Daniel?
Express your answer in years and months.

39 months ⟨
36 months = 3 years
3 months

+ 12 + 12 + 12
12, 24, 36, 48

39 months = 3 years + ☐ months

= 3 years ☐ months

9 years 5 months + ☐ years ☐ months = ☐ years ☐ months

Daniel is ☐ years ☐ months old.

☑ 1. Understand
☑ 2. Plan
☑ 3. Answer
☑ 4. Check

Let's Do

1. Zack took 4 weeks 5 days to complete a Science project.
    Maria took 11 fewer days to complete the same Science project.
    How long did Maria take to complete the Science project?
    Express your answer in days.

4 weeks 5 days ⟨
4 weeks = _____ days
_____ days

1 week = 7 days

4 weeks 5 days = _____ days + _____ days

= _____ days

_____ days − 11 days = _____ days

Maria took _____ days to complete
the Science project.

☐ 1. Understand
☐ 2. Plan
☐ 3. Answer
☐ 4. Check

P/B Chapter 12: Exercise 8, pages 119–121

Practice 3

1. The flight time from Singapore to Bangkok is 1 hour 45 minutes and from Singapore to Manila is 3 h 15 min.
   How much longer does it take to fly to Manila than to Bangkok?

2. Mr. Li and his family went to the beach for a picnic.
   They left home at 8:30 a.m. and arrived at the beach at 9:15 a.m.
   How long did the journey take?

3. A supermarket opens for business at 9:30 a.m.
   Its workers have to report for work 40 minutes earlier.
   What time must the workers report for work?

4. A bookshop is open from 9:00 a.m. to 5:00 p.m. every day.

   a) How long is the bookshop open each day?
   b) How long is the bookshop open in a week?

5. Chandran and Mohan took 2 hours 30 minutes each to clean up their rooms.
   Chandran finished cleaning his room at 9:20 a.m.
   Mohan started cleaning his room 1 hour 30 minutes later.
   What time did Mohan finish cleaning his room?

6. A group of children left for an excursion at 8:30 a.m.
   They returned to school 4 hours 10 minutes later.
   They took a short break in school before going home at 1:25 p.m. How long was the break?

7. Fernando took 2 years 3 months to save some money to buy a computer.
   Lila took 8 months less to save for the same computer.
   How long did Lila take to save the money needed?
   Express your answer in months.

8. Sharon spent 2 weeks 5 days on holiday in Australia.
   Her sister, Nadia, decided to stay on for 6 more days.
   How long did Nadia stay in Australia?
   Express your answer in weeks and days.

Mind stretcher

Let's Learn

Kelly is 9 years old. Her brother, Ryan, is 29 years old.
How many years later will Ryan's age be twice Kelly's age?

1 **Understand** the problem.

How old is Kelly now?
How old is Ryan now?
What do I need to find?

2 **Plan** what to do.

I can **draw a bar model**.

3 Work out the **Answer**.

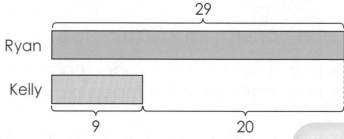

The difference in age between Kelly and Ryan is 20 years.

When Ryan's age is twice that of Kelly's age:

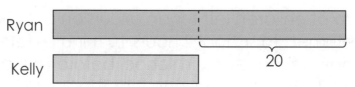

The difference in age will always remain the same.

$20 \times 2 = 40$
Ryan will be 40 years old when he is twice Kelly's age.
$40 - 29 = 11$
Ryan will be twice Kelly's age 11 years later.

4 **Check**
Did you answer the question? Is your answer correct?

$9 + 11 = 20$
Kelly will be 20 years old 11 years later.
$40 \div 20 = 2$
Ryan will be twice Kelly's age.
My answer is correct.

134

13 Geometry

Lesson 1   Angles

You will learn to...
- identify and name points, lines, line segments and rays
- identify angles in objects and shapes
- compare sizes of angles

Identifying and naming points, lines, line segments and rays

Let's Learn

a)   A **point** shows an exact location.

•
P

This is a point. We name it Point P.

A point is represented by a dot.

b)   A **line** is a straight path that extends endlessly in both directions.
It has no endpoints.

This line passes through points P and Q.
We name it Line PQ or Line QP.

c)   A **line segment** is part of a line.
It has two endpoints.

A line segment does not extend endlessly.

This line segment has endpoints P and Q.
We name it Line segment PQ or Line segment QP.

d) A **ray** is part of a line.
It has one endpoint and extends
endlessly in one direction.

This ray has an endpoint P and passes
through Point Q.
We can name it Ray PQ.

Let's Do

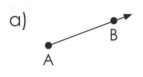

1. Name the diagrams.

a)

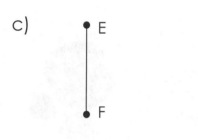

_____

b)

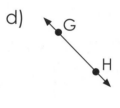

C

_____

c)

E

F

_____

d)

G

H

_____

Identifying angles

Let's Learn

a) An **angle** can be formed by two rays with a
common endpoint.

This angle is formed by the rays OP and OQ.
The common endpoint is O.

136

b) An angle can also be formed by two line segments with a common endpoint.

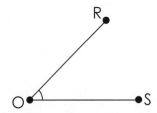

This angle is formed by the line segments OR and OS.
The common endpoint is O.

Let's Do

1. Circle the diagrams that show an angle.

a)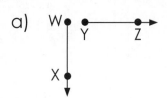

b)

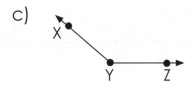

c)

d)

P/B Chapter 13: Exercise 1, pages 122–123

Comparing sizes of angles

Let's Learn

 a) Fold a card in half to form an angle as shown.

Then, form a bigger angle.
What is the biggest angle you can form?
Compare it with your friends.

b)

A   **B**   **C**

Which angle is the smallest? ▢

Which angle is the biggest? ▢

Let's Do

1. Look at the angles formed by the craft sticks.

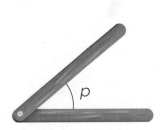 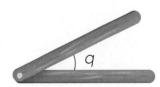 

a) Which angle is the smallest? _q_

b) Which angle is the biggest? _r_

P/B Chapter 13: Exercise 2, page 124

Identifying angles on objects

Here are some examples of angles found on objects.

Look for more angles on objects around you.

Let's Do

1. Mark two angles on each object.

    a)

    b)

    c)

P/B Chapter 13: Exercise 3, page 125

Identifying angles in shapes

Let's Learn

a) Look at the triangle.
Two sides of a triangle meet to form an angle.

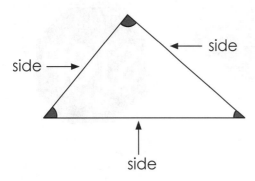

side

side

side

The triangle has 3 sides and 3 angles.

b) Look at the square.

The square has **4** sides
and **4** angles.

The sides of a square
meet to form angles.

Let's Do

1. Look at each shape.

a) Mark the angles of each shape.
Write the number of sides and angles.

_4_ sides

_4_ angles

_6_ sides

_6_ angles

_8_ sides

_8_ angles

b) What do you notice about the number of sides and the
number of angles of each shape?

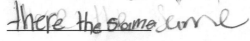

there the same sorne

P/B Chapter 13: Exercise 4, page 126

Practice 1

1. Which of the following is a ray?

   a)  P Q

   b) • P

   c) •——————• P Q

2. Which of the following is a line segment?

   a)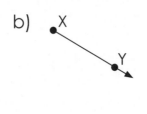

   b)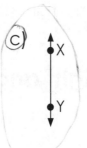

   c)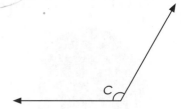

3.

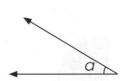 a   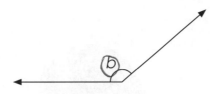 b   c

   a) Which angle is the biggest? b

   b) Which angle is the smallest? a

4. Mark an angle on each object.

   a)    b)    c)

5. Mark two angles on each shape.

   a) 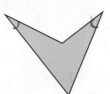   b)

6. How many sides and angles does each shape have?

 A   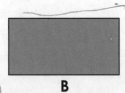 B   C   D

A: 3 angles 3 sides   B: 4 angles and 4 sides   C: 4 angles and 4 sides   D: 6 angles and 6 sides

141

Lesson 2   Right Angles

You will learn to...
- identify right angles
- tell whether a given angle is equal to, smaller than or bigger than a right angle

Identifying right angles

Let's Learn

Fold a piece of paper to make an angle as shown.

The corner of the folded piece of paper is a **right angle**.

Use the folded piece of paper to check for right angles.

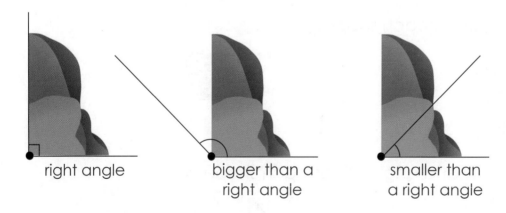

right angle   bigger than a   smaller than
                     right angle   a right angle

1. a) Use the folded piece of paper to find out which of the following angles are right angles.
        Circle your answer.

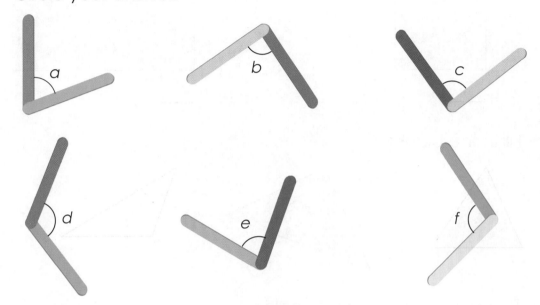

    b) Which angles are bigger than a right angle? _____

    c) Which angles are smaller than a right angle? _____

P/B Chapter 13: Exercise 5, page 127

Identifying right angles in shapes

Let's Learn

Use the folded piece of paper to check for the right angles in Triangle A.

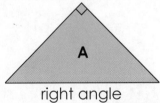

right angle

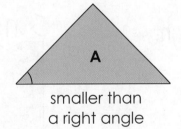

smaller than a right angle

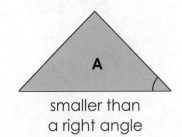

smaller than a right angle

Triangle A has 1 right angle and 2 angles smaller than a right angle.

143

1. Write the number of right angles in each shape.

   a)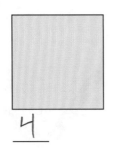

   <u>4</u>

   b)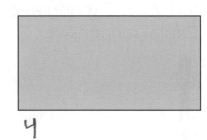

   <u>4</u>

2. Fill in the blanks.

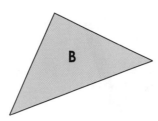
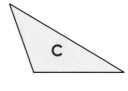

Triangle <u>B</u> has a right angle.

Triangle <u>C</u> has an angle bigger than a right angle.

P/B Chapter 13: Exercise 6, pages 128–129

Practice 2

1. How many angles does each of these figures have?
   How many are right angles?

   a) 4 angles a 1 right angles
   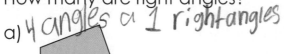

   P
   3

   b) 5 angles and 1 right ang

   Q
   5

   c) 4 angles and 2 right angles
   R
   2

   d) 5 angles and 2 right an
   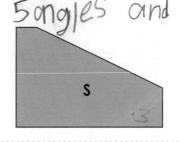

   S
   3

Lesson 3　Problem Solving

Mind stretcher

Let's Learn

The numbers below are formed with craft sticks.

a)

b)

Move only 1 craft stick in each number to form a new number.
Keep the number of right angles the same.

1 **Understand** the problem.

> What numbers are given?
> How many craft sticks make each number?
> How many right angles are there in each number?

2 **Plan** what to do.

> I can **act it out**.

3 Work out the **Answer**.

a)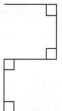

b)

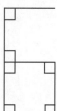

4 **Check**
Did you answer the question?
Are your answers correct?

> The number of craft sticks and the number of right angles have not changed.
> My answers are correct.

☑ 1. Understand
☑ 2. Plan
☑ 3. Answer
☑ 4. Check

PB Review 6, pages 130–137

Perpendicular and Parallel Line Segments

1. We can draw figures on a square grid.
   Copy the figure on the square grid.

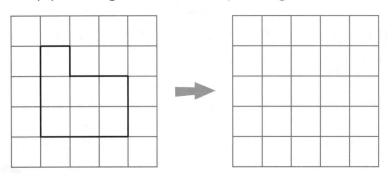

We can copy the same figure onto another square grid.

2. A line segment is part of a line.
   It has two endpoints.

This line segment has endpoints Y and Z.
We can name it Line segment YZ or Line segment ZY.

3.

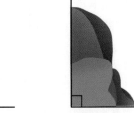

Mark ⌐ to show that the angle is a right angle.

Angle *x* is a right angle.
A folded piece of paper can be used to check
for a right angle.

Lesson 1   Perpendicular Line Segments

You will learn to...
- identify perpendicular line segments
- draw perpendicular line segments on a square grid

Identifying perpendicular line segments

Let's Learn

a)   Here are some examples of **perpendicular** line segments found on objects around us.

We mark a right angle to show perpendicular lines.

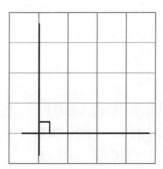 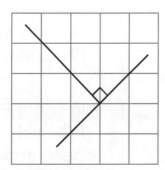 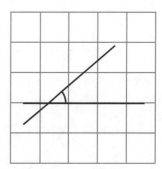

These two line segments are perpendicular. They cross at right angles.

These two line segments are perpendicular. They meet at a right angle.

These two line segments are not perpendicular. They do not cross at right angles.

Look for more examples of perpendicular line segments around you.

Place a folded piece of paper over each angle to check whether it is a right angle.

b)

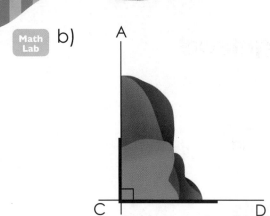

Line segment AB is perpendicular to Line segment CD.
We write AB ⊥ CD.

⊥ stands for
is perpendicular to.

c)   Look at the figures below.
Use the folded piece of paper to check for right angles where the line segments meet.

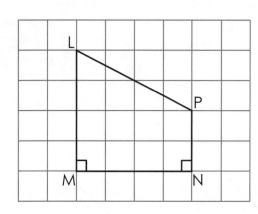

In figure LMNP, Line segment LM and Line segment MN are perpendicular to each other.
LM ⊥ MN

Line segments PN and MN are perpendicular to each other.
PN ⊥ NM

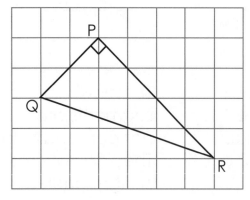

In figure PQR, Line segment PQ and Line segment PR are perpendicular to each other.
PQ ⊥ PR

Which line segments are not perpendicular to each other?

1. Mark a right angle if the line segments are perpendicular.

   a)
   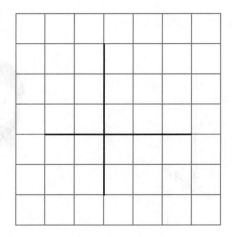

   b)
   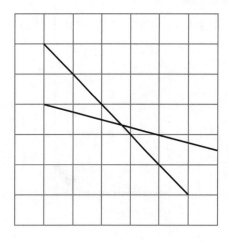

2. Which line segment is perpendicular to Line segment PQ?

   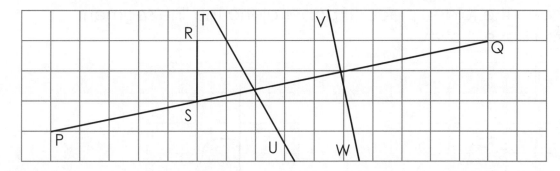

   _____

3. Name one pair of perpendicular line segments in each figure.

   a)
   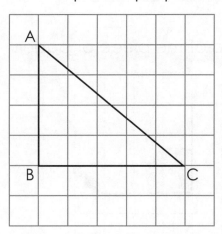

   b)
   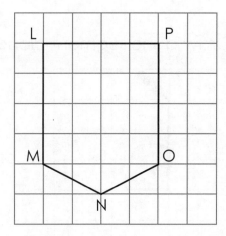

   _____   _____

Chapter 14: Exercise 1, pages 138–140

Drawing perpendicular line segments

a) Draw a line segment along any of the grid lines on the square grid.

Use a ruler.

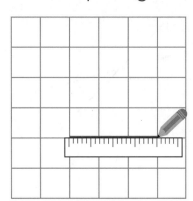   or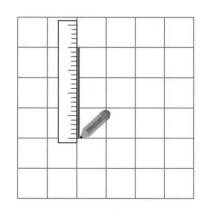

Place the folded piece of paper along the line segment you have drawn.

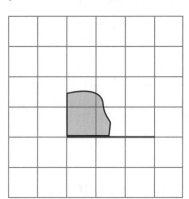   or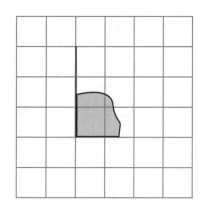

Draw a line segment along the fold of the piece of paper.

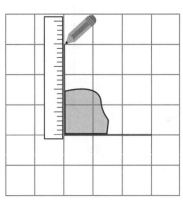   or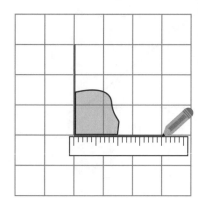

150

b) Draw a line segment as shown.

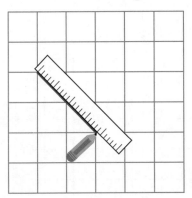   or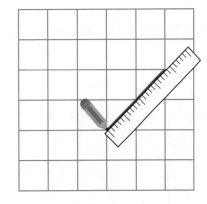

Place the folded piece of paper along the line segment you have drawn.

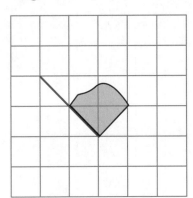   or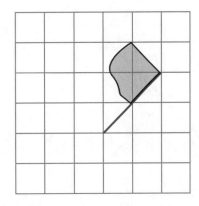

Draw a line segment along the fold of the piece of paper.

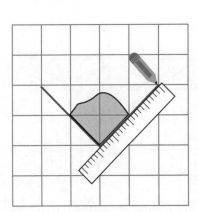   or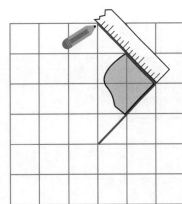

1. Copy the perpendicular line segments onto the grid.

a)

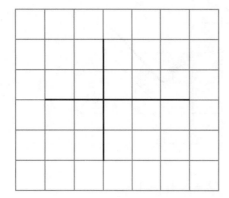

b)

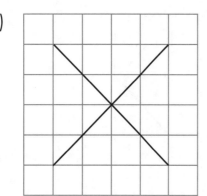

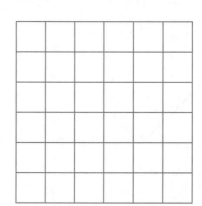

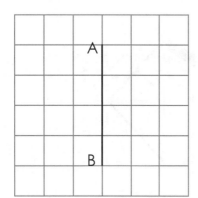

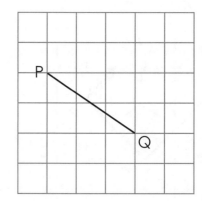

2. Draw a line segment perpendicular to the line segment given.

a)

b)

P/B Chapter 14: Exercise 2, pages 141–142

Practice 1

1. State which line segments are perpendicular using the symbol ⊥.

a)

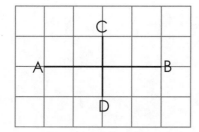

b)

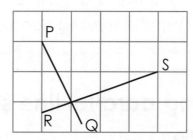

c)

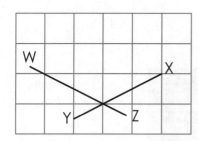

d)

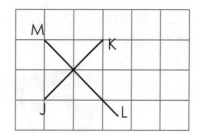

2. Draw two line segments perpendicular to the line segment given.

a)

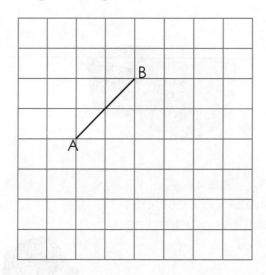

b)

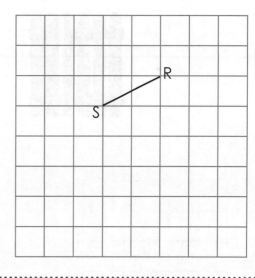

Lesson 2   Parallel Line Segments

You will learn to...
- identify parallel line segments
- draw parallel line segments on a square grid

Identifying parallel line segments

Let's Learn

a)   Here are some examples of **parallel** line segments found on objects around us.

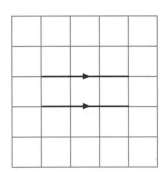

Mark ▸ on both lines to show parallel lines.

These two line segments are parallel.
They are always the same distance apart.
They will never meet.

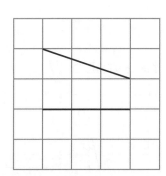

The line segments will meet at a point if we draw them longer.

These two line segments are not parallel. They are not always the same distance apart.

These two line segments are not parallel. They cross each other at one point.

Look for more examples of parallel line segments around you.

b) We can count the number of square units between the lines on a grid to check if two lines are parallel.

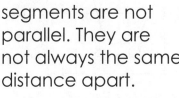

Line segment AB is always 2 square units away from Line segment CD.
So, Line segment AB is parallel to Line segment CD.
We write Line segment AB // Line segment CD.

// means **is parallel to**.

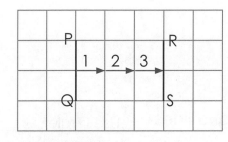

Line segment PQ is always 3 square units away from Line segment RS. So, Line segment PQ is parallel to Line segment RS. We write Line segment PQ // Line segment RS.

c)

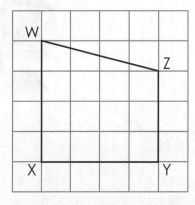

In Figure WXYZ, Line segments WX and ZY are parallel to each other.
WX // ZY

Are Line segments WX and XY parallel or perpendicular to each other?
Explain why.

1. Name the pairs of parallel line segments. Use the symbol //.

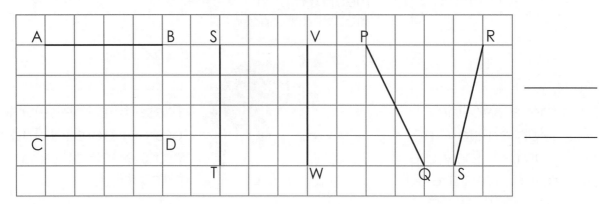

_____

_____

2. Name one pair of parallel line segments in each figure.
   Use the symbol //.

a)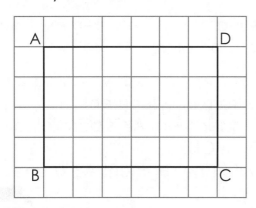

b)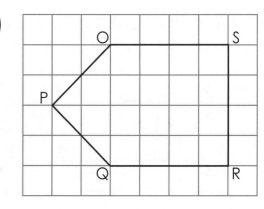

_____

_____

P/B Chapter 14: Exercise 3, pages 143–145

Drawing parallel line segments

Let's Learn

a) Draw a line segment along any of the grid lines on the square grid.

Use a ruler.

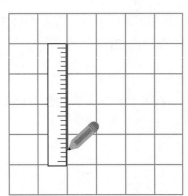

or

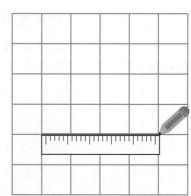

Draw another line segment along the grid lines
1 or more units away.

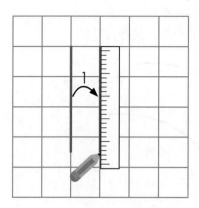 or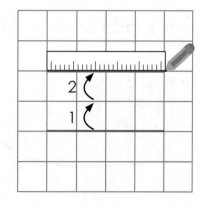

b) Draw a line segment as shown.

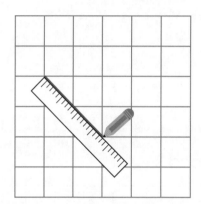 or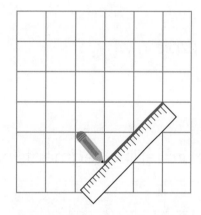

Draw another line segment 1 or more units away.

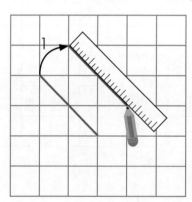 or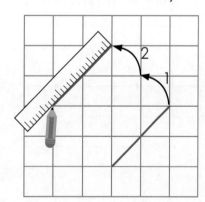

Yen walks along this road from her home to school daily.

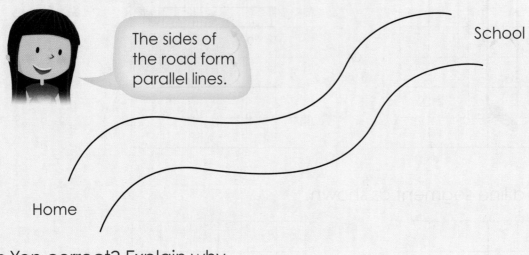

Is Yen correct? Explain why.

Let's Do

1. Copy the parallel line segments onto the grid.

a)

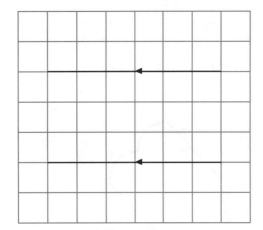

b)

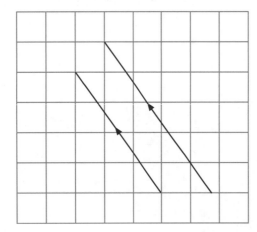

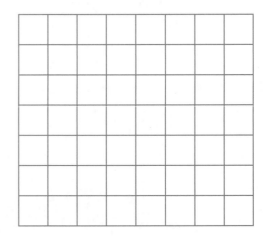

2. Draw a line segment parallel to the line segment given.

a)

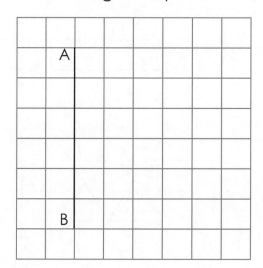

b)

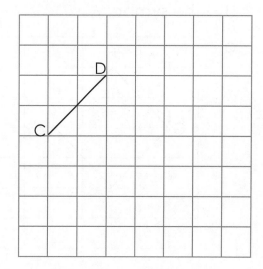

P/B Chapter 14: Exercise 4, pages 146–147

Practice 2

1. Tell if the line segments are parallel.

a)

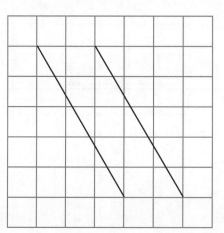

b)

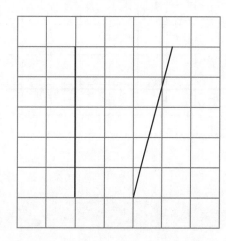

c)

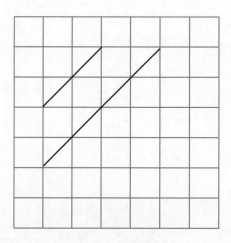

d)

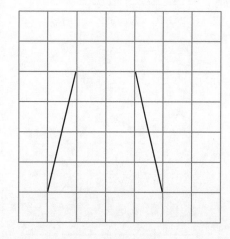

2. Name the parallel line segments in each figure.
Use the symbol //.

a)

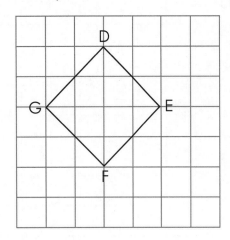

b)

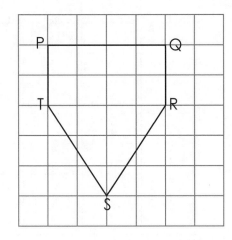

3. Draw a line segment parallel to the line segment given.

a)

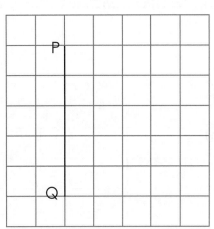

b)

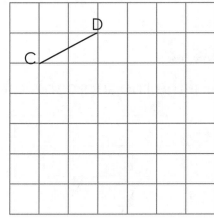

Lesson 3 Horizontal and Vertical Line Segments

You will learn to...
- identify horizontal and vertical line segments

Horizontal and vertical line segments

Math Lab

Picture It

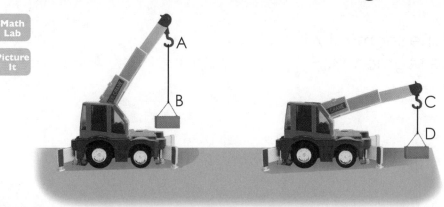

AB and CD are **vertical** line segments.

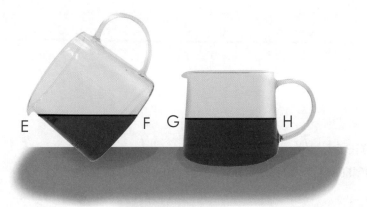

EF and GH are **horizontal** line segments.

Look around you.
Find other vertical and
horizontal line segments.

All vertical line segments are parallel to one another.
All horizontal line segments are parallel to one another.

All vertical line segments meet or cross horizontal line segments at a right angle.
So, a vertical line segment and a horizontal line segment are perpendicular to each other.

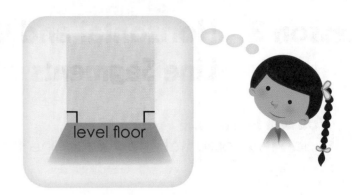

level floor

Let's Do

1. Name the horizontal line segment AB.
    Name the vertical line segment YZ.

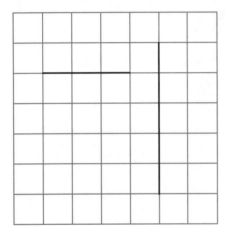

Practice 3

1. Name the vertical line segment WX.
    Name the horizontal line segment XY.

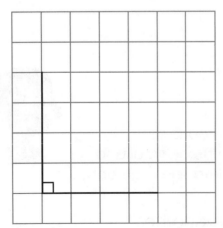

Lesson 4 Problem Solving

Mind stretcher

Let's Learn

In the figure below, ABCD is a rectangle and BCEF is a square. How many pairs of perpendicular line segments are there in the figure?

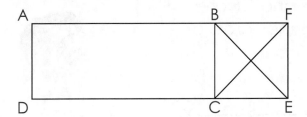

1 Understand the problem.

What are the shapes in the figure? What do I have to find?

2 Plan what to do.

I can **simplify the problem** by first looking at each shape individually.

3 Work out the Answer.

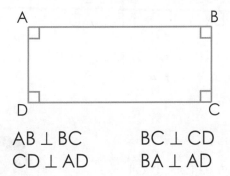

Perpendicular line segments meet or cross at a right angle.

AB ⊥ BC   BC ⊥ CD
CD ⊥ AD   BA ⊥ AD

There are 4 pairs of perpendicular line segments.

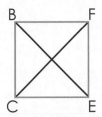

The 4 sides of the square meet at right angles. So, we know that it has 4 pairs of perpendicular line segments like the rectangle.

163

BF ⊥ FE   FE ⊥ EC
CE ⊥ BC   BC ⊥ BF

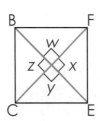

Use a folded piece of paper to check any one of the angles between line segments BE and CF.

Line segments BE and CF are perpendicular as they cross at a right angle.
BE ⊥ CF

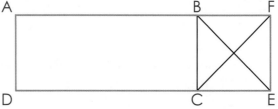

Putting the two shapes together, we have a bigger rectangle with 4 sides meeting at right angles.

AD ⊥ DE   DE ⊥ EF
EF ⊥ FA   AF ⊥ AD

Total number of perpendicular line segments
= 4 + 4 + 1 + 4
= 13

 Check
Did you answer the question? Is your answer correct?

I have found all the perpendicular line segments in the figure. My answer is correct.

☑ 1. Understand
☑ 2. Plan
☑ 3. Answer
☑ 4. Check

Area

Lesson 1 Square Units

You will learn ...
- the meaning of area
- to measure area in units
- to compare the areas of figures made up of squares and half squares

Square units

Let's Learn

a) These figures are made up of square tiles.

Each figure is made up of 6 square tiles.
The figures have different shapes, but they have the **same size**.
They have the same **area**.

The area of each figure is 6 **square units**.

Each [tile] is 1 square unit.

b)

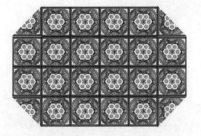

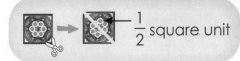

$\frac{1}{2}$ square unit

The area of the figure is 22 square units.

Let's Do

1. Use square cards to make these shapes.

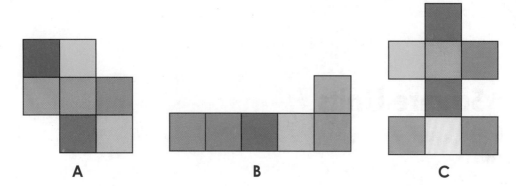

A   B   C

The area of Shape A is ____ square units.

The area of Shape B is ____ square units.

The area of Shape C is ____ square units.

Shape ____ is the biggest.

Shape ____ is the smallest.

2. Which two shapes are of the same size? ____ and ____

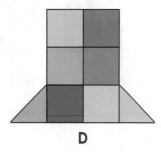

D

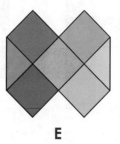

E

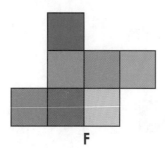

F

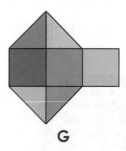

G

P/B Chapter 15: Exercises 1–2, pages 148–152

Understanding area

Let's Learn

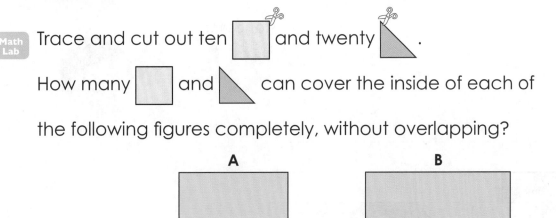

Math Lab Trace and cut out ten ▢ and twenty ◣.

How many ▢ and ◣ can cover the inside of each of

the following figures completely, without overlapping?

A   B

Figure A ▢
Figure B ▢

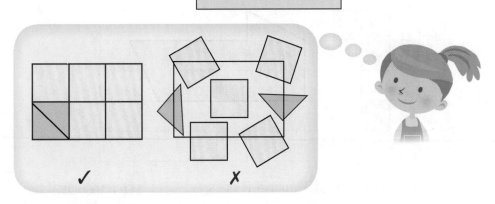

✓   ✗

The area of a figure is the number of square units needed to cover the surface of the figure.

Which figure has a greater area? ▢

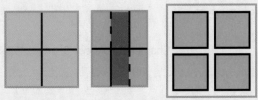

These figures are each covered by four square tiles.
Do they have the same area? Explain why.

1. What is the area of each of the following figures?

Each ☐ stands for 1 square unit.

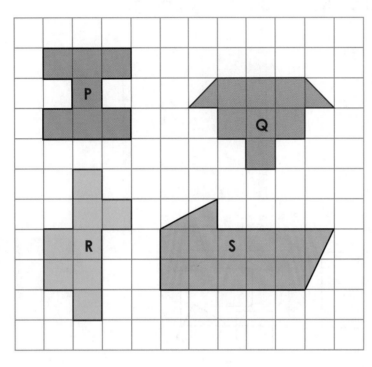

a) The area of Figure P is _____ square units.

b) The area of Figure Q is _____ square units.

c) The area of Figure R is _____ square units.

d) The area of Figure S is _____ square units.

e) Figure _____ and Figure _____ have the same area.

f) Figure _____ has the greatest area.

g) Figure _____ has the smallest area.

P/B Chapter 15: Exercise 3, pages 153–154

Practice 1

1. a) What is the area of each of the figures?

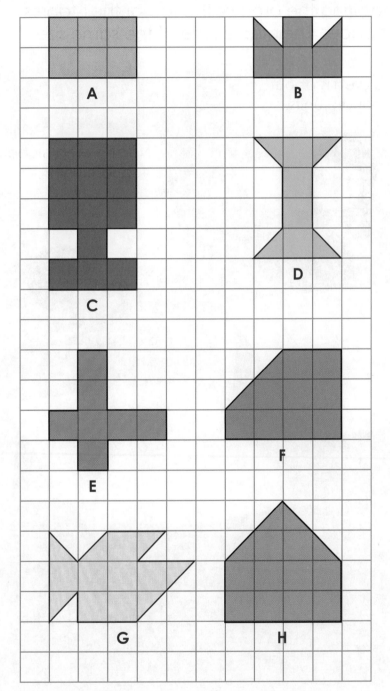

   b) Which figure has the smallest area?

   c) Which figure has the greatest area?

   d) Which figures have the same area?

Yen and Sam are measuring the area of the top of their tables with square pieces of paper. Their tables are of the same size.

Who is correct? Explain why.

Lesson 2   Area in Square Centimeters and Square Meters

You will learn ...
- to find the area of figures made up of 1-centimeter or 1-meter squares and half squares
- to compare the areas of figures made up of 1-centimeter or 1-meter squares

Area of squares in square centimeters

Let's Learn

This is a 1-centimeter square.

Each side of the square is 1 centimeter long.

Its area is 1 **square centimeter**.
The square centimeter is a unit of area.
We write square centimeter as **cm²**.

What is the area of these squares?

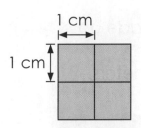

2-centimeter square

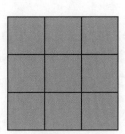

3-centimeter square

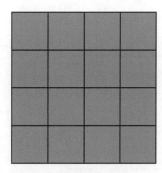

4-centimeter square

How do I find the area of these squares?

One way to find the area of squares is shown below.

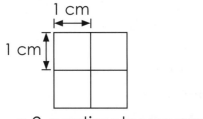

a 2-centimeter square

A 2-centimeter square is made up of 4 pieces of 1-centimeter squares. Its area is 4 square centimeters.

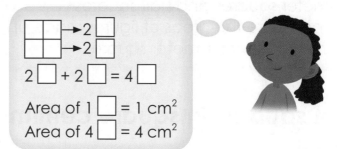

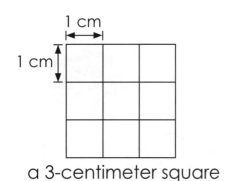

a 3-centimeter square

A 3-centimeter square is made up of ▓ 1-centimeter squares. Its area is ▓ square centimeters.

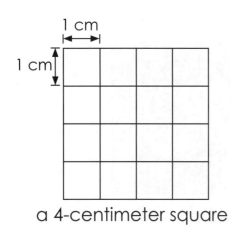

a 4-centimeter square

A 4-centimeter square is made up of ▓ 1-centimeter squares. Its area is ▓ square centimeters.

Let's Do

1. a) What is the area of a 5-centimeter square?

    b) What is the area of a 10-centimeter square?

Area of other figures in square centimeters

Let's Learn

Picture It

This figure is made up of 1-centimeter squares.
What is its area?

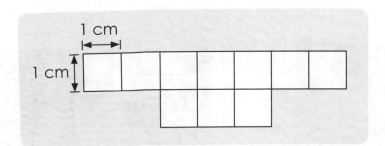

The figure is made up of 10 1-centimeter squares.
Its area is 10 square centimeters.

Let's Do

1. Fill in the blanks.

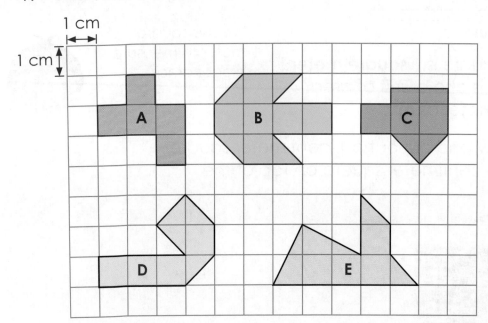

a) The area of Figure D is ____ square centimeters.

b) The area of Figure E is ____ square centimeters.

c) Figure ____ and Figure ____ have the same area.

d) Figure ____ has the greatest area.

P/B Chapter 15: Exercises 4–5, pages 155–157

Understanding square meters

Paste a few pieces of newspaper together.
Then, measure 1 meter on each side and cut out a square.

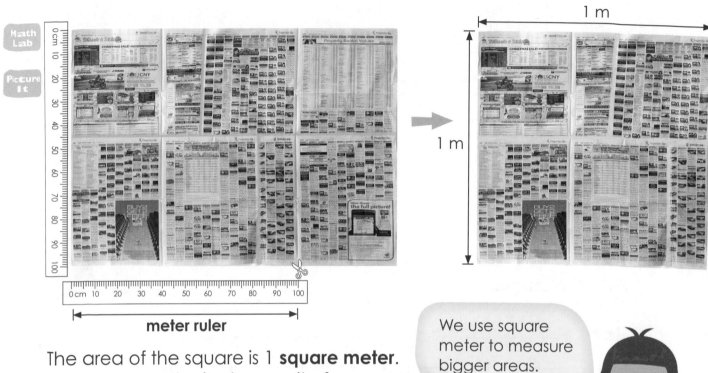

meter ruler

The area of the square is 1 **square meter**.
The square meter is also a unit of area.
We write square meter as **m²**.

We use square meter to measure bigger areas.

Use a ruler to draw and cut out a 1-centimeter square.
Then, place the 1-centimeter square on top of the
1-meter square.
Compare the sizes.

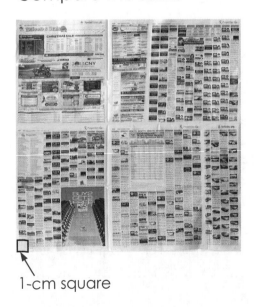

1-cm square

Area in square meters

Give the area of each of the figures in square meters.

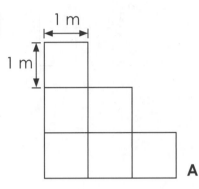

A

Figure A is made up of 6 1-meter squares.
Its area is 6 square meters.

Area of 1 ☐ = 1 m²
Area of 6 ☐ = 6 m²

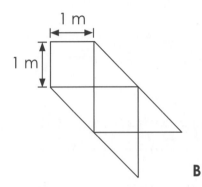

B

Figure B is made up of ▓ 1-meter squares.
Its area is ▓ square meters.

◨ = ☐

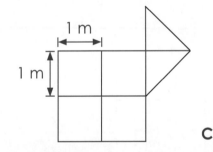

C

Figure C is made up of ▓ 1-meter squares.
Its area is ▓ square meters.

Let's Do

1. Use a 1-meter square to estimate the area of your classroom floor. What other things can you find in your classroom that have an area of about 1 square meter?

2. Fill in the blanks with **square centimeters** or **square meters**.

    a) The area of a table top is about 2 _____.

    b) The area of this page is about 600 _____.

    c) The area of a stamp is about 4 _____.

3. Fill in the blanks.

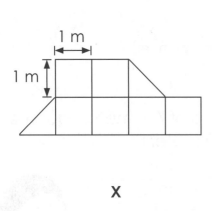

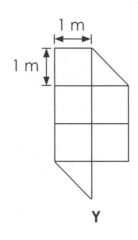

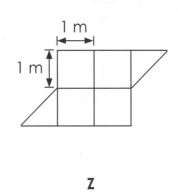

X   Y   Z

a) The area of Figure X is ____ square meters.

b) The area of Figure Y is ____ square meters.

c) The area of Figure Z is ____ square meters.

d) Figure ____ has the greatest area.

P/B Chapter 15: Exercises 6–7, pages 158–159

Practice 2

1.

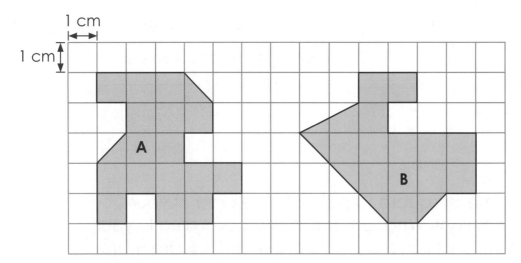

a) What is the area of Figure A?

b) What is the area of Figure B?

c) Which has a greater area, Figure A or Figure B?

2. a) What is the area of a 6-centimeter square?

   b) What is the area of a 7-centimeter square?

   c) What is the area of an 8-centimeter square?

3. Fill in the blanks.

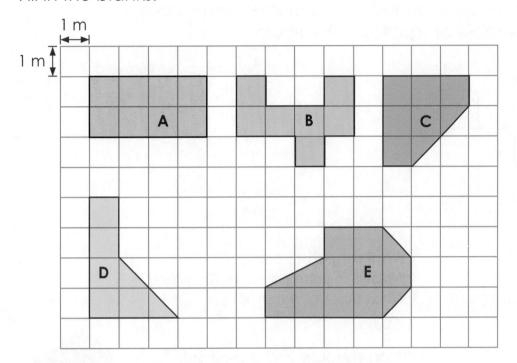

   a) Which two figures have the same area?

   b) Which figure has the greatest area?

   c) Which figure has the smallest area?

Lesson 3   Problem Solving

Mind stretcher

Let's Learn

The figure below is formed by 1-centimeter squares.
Find the number of squares in the figure.

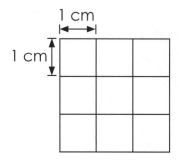

1 Understand the problem.

What shape is the figure?
What is the size given for the figure?
What do I have to find?

2 Plan what to do.

I can **visualize** and **draw it out**.

3 Work out the Answer.

1-centimeter square

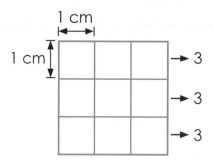

$3 \times 3 = 9$

There are nine 1-centimeter squares.

2-centimeter square

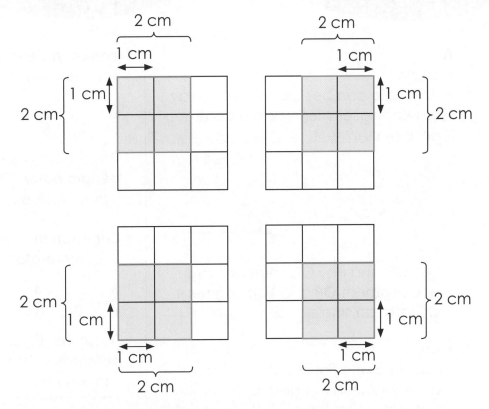

There are four 2-centimeter squares.

3-centimeter square

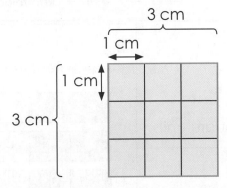

There is one 3-centimeter square.
So, there are 9 + 4 + 1 = 14
squares in all.

4 **Check**
Did you answer
the question?
Is your answer
correct?

There are nine 1-centimeter
squares, four 2-centimeter
squares and one 3-centimeter
square. I have found the number
of squares in the given figure.
My answer is correct.

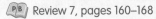
☑ 1. Understand
☑ 2. Plan
☑ 3. Answer
☑ 4. Check

P/B Review 7, pages 160–168

Glossary

A

- **angle**

  An **angle** can be formed by two rays or two line segments with a common endpoint.

  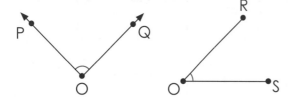

  Ray OP and Ray OQ form an angle. Line segment OR and Line segment OS form an angle.

- **area**

  The **area** of a figure is the number of square units needed to cover the surface of the figure.

  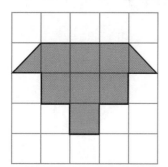

  The area of the figure is 8 square units.

C

- **capacity**

  The **capacity** of a container is the amount it can hold when full. The capacity of the bottle is 1 liter.

- **common denominator**

  See **denominator**.

  $$\frac{1}{5} \quad \frac{3}{5} \quad \frac{4}{5}$$

  These fractions have a **common denominator**. The denominator is the same number.

- **common numerator**

  See **numerator**.

  $$\frac{3}{4} \quad \frac{3}{8} \quad \frac{3}{10}$$

  These fractions have a **common numerator**. The numerator is the same number.

D

- **denominator**

  $$\frac{3}{4} \longleftarrow \text{denominator}$$

E

- **equivalent fractions**

  | $\frac{1}{2}$ | $\frac{1}{2}$ |

  | $\frac{1}{4}$ | $\frac{1}{4}$ | $\frac{1}{4}$ | $\frac{1}{4}$ |

  | $\frac{1}{8}$ | $\frac{1}{8}$ | $\frac{1}{8}$ | $\frac{1}{8}$ | $\frac{1}{8}$ | $\frac{1}{8}$ | $\frac{1}{8}$ | $\frac{1}{8}$ |

  $$\frac{1}{2} = \frac{2}{4} = \frac{4}{8}$$

  $\frac{1}{2}, \frac{2}{4}$ and $\frac{4}{8}$ are **equivalent fractions**. They have different numerators and denominators, but are equal.

H

• horizontal

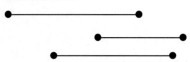

These line segments are **horizontal.**

K

• kilometer (km)

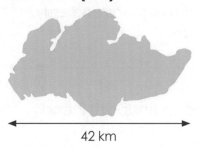

42 km

Use **kilometer** to measure long distances.

L

• like fractions
*See **common denominator**.*

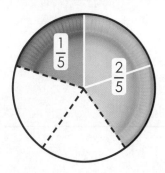

Like fractions have the same denominator.

• line
A **line** is a straight path extending endlessly in both directions with no endpoints.

P   Q

Line PQ passes through points P and Q.

• line segment
A **line segment** is part of a line with two endpoints.

P   Q

Line segment PQ has endpoints P and Q.

• liter (L)

There is 1 **liter** of liquid in the beaker.
Use liter to measure greater volumes.

M

• milliliter (ml)

There are 200 **milliliters** of liquid in the beaker.
Use milliliter to measure smaller volumes.

• millimeter (mm)

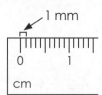

Use **millimeter** to measure the length of very short objects.

N

- **numerator**

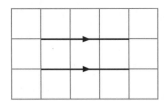

$$\frac{3}{4} \longleftarrow \text{numerator}$$

P

- **parallel (//)**

These two line segments are **parallel**. They are always the same distance apart and will never meet.

- **past**

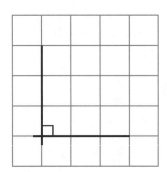

The time is 10 minutes **past** 12. It is 12:10.

- **perpendicular (⊥)**
  See right angle.

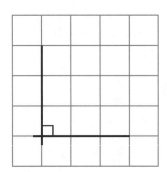

These two line segments are **perpendicular**. They cross at a right angle.

- **point**

  A **point** shows an exact location.

  •
  P

  This is Point P.

R

- **ray**

  A ray is part of a line with one endpoint and extends endlessly in one direction.

Ray PQ has an endpoint P and passes through Point Q.

- **right angle**
  See angle, perpendicular.
  A **right angle** is formed by two perpendicular lines.

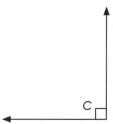

Angle c is a right angle.

S

- **simplest form**

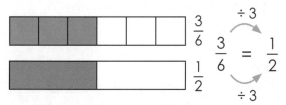

$\frac{1}{2}$ is the **simplest form** of $\frac{3}{6}$.

The numerator and denominator cannot be further divided by the same number.

- **square centimeter (cm²)**

The area of the square is 1 **square centimeter**.

- **square meter (m²)**

The area of the square is 1 **square meter**.

- **square unit**

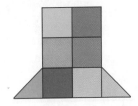

The area of the figure is 7 **square units**.

T

- **to**

The time is 15 minutes **to** 11.
It is 10:45.

V

- **vertical**

These line segments are **vertical**.

- **volume**

The **volume** of liquid in a container is the amount of space it takes up. The volume of liquid in the beaker is 200 milliliters.

Problem Solving Process

Solve problems using these 4 steps:

1 **Understand** the problem.
Can you describe the problem in your own words?
- What information is given?
- What do you need to find?
- Is there information that is missing or not needed?

2 **Plan** what to do.
What can you do to help you solve the problem?
Here are some things you can do:
- Draw a picture
- Make a list
- Choose an operation
- Guess and check
- Look for a pattern
- Act it out
- Work backwards
- Solve part of the problem

3 Work out the **Answer**.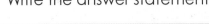
Solve the problem using your plan in Step 2.
If you cannot solve the problem, make another plan.
Show your work clearly.
Write the answer statement.

4 **Check**
Read the question again. Did you answer the question?
Does your answer make sense?
Is your answer correct?
You may use the following to help you check your answer:
- fact families
- replace the unknown in the problem with your answer
If your answer is not correct, go back to Step 1.